857

ROSE MACAULAY

In 1957 Constance Babington Smith wrote her first book *Evidence in Camera: The Story of Photographic Intelligence in World War II*, and this was followed by *Testing Time: A Study of Man and Machine in the Test Flying Era*.

Soon after the death of her cousin Rose Macaulay she was invited to edit her letters, and between 1961 and 1964 three volumes of these were published as *Letters to a Friend*, *Last Letters to a Friend* and *Letters to a Sister*. She has also edited Rose Macaulay's *Pleasure of Ruins*, for an edition with photographs by Roloff Beny.

In 1967 she published *Amy Johnson* the biography of Britain's pioneer woman aviator.

Rose Macaulay

CONSTANCE BABINGTON SMITH

COLLINS
St James's Place, London

William Collins Sons & Co Ltd
London · Glasgow · Sydney · Auckland
Toronto · Johannesburg

First published 1972
First reprint 1973
© Constance Babington Smith 1972

ISBN 0 00 211720 7

Set in Monotype Bembo
Made and printed in Great Britain by
William Collins Sons & Company Ltd Glasgow

CONTENTS

CONTENTS

ILLUSTRATIONS

PREFACE

Not all writers rate a biography, but Rose Macaulay was no ordinary writer. She was poet, journalist, historian, anthologist, broadcaster, letter-writer, as well as the author of many novels. Furthermore her life was full of activity, interest and exceptional friendships, and in many ways it throws light on her most important writings.

Central to her life was her love for a married man who died in 1942. This was made clear in letters which she wrote, some years later, to an Anglican priest, Father Hamilton Johnson. After her death I became responsible for all her writings, and it was decided, in consultation with her sister Jean, the only surviving member of her immediate family, that the letters to Father Johnson should be published. When they appeared a controversy arose. Some thought that Rose herself would not have approved. But in the instructions she left, as regards the disposal of her papers, she had not specified that any of her own letters should be destroyed or kept secret. And it may be added that Father Johnson's purpose in initiating the idea of publication – the aim of helping others – has been vindicated by the gratitude of many readers.

In the two books of Rose's letters to Father Johnson, published in 1961 and 1962, the identity of her 'beloved companion' was withheld because his widow was still alive. She has since died, and his name, Gerald O'Donovan, is included in the present book.

I am deeply grateful to Jean Macaulay for her help and encouragement at every stage of my work on the book, and also to Rose's friends who have lent me letters and assisted me in many ways. I am glad that some of their own tributes, which first appeared in *Encounter* under the heading 'The Pleasures of Knowing Rose Macaulay' should be included as an appendix.

Constance Babington Smith

Cambridge
April 1972

ACKNOWLEDGEMENTS

A number of Rose Macaulay's relatives, in addition to her sister Jean, have helped me in various ways, and I want to express my gratitude to Miss Dorothea Conybeare who made letters available, Mrs Donald Macaulay who shared her memories with me, Miss F. M. McCormick who lent me diaries and other material, Lady Fletcher and Mrs Tom Cain who allowed me to quote from letters, and Miss Elizabeth Hamilton Smith and Sir Roger Chance who loaned me photographs.

During recent years many friends of Rose Macaulay's have talked and written of her to me; I am especially indebted to the late Miss Marjorie Grant Cook and the late Lady Nicholson. In addition I would like to mention Miss Elizabeth Bowen, Mrs Guy Chapman, the late Dame Myra Curtis, Mr Eric Gillett, Lady Gollancz, Mr Hamish Hamilton, Miss Esther Heacock, the Rev. Gerard Irvine, Mr Laurie Lee, Miss Rosamond Lehmann, the Rev. Denis Marsh, s.s.f., Mr Ernest Milton, Lady Ross, Herr Helmut Rückriegel, Miss Lucie Savill, the late Mr H. B. Usher and Mrs Usher, and the late Miss Olive Willis. Others to whom I am grateful for facilitating my researches are Mr Alan Babington Smith, Mrs Quentin Bell, Professor Alice Bensen, Mrs H. Cohen, Mr Nicholas Furbank, Mrs Peter Grain, Mrs M. I. Hamblin-Smith and Mr Andrew Stewart-Roberts, as well as the Librarian of the Cambridge University Library, the Keeper of Western Manuscripts in the Bodleian Library, the Principal of Somerville College, Oxford, the Headmistress of the Oxford High School, the General Secretary of International P.E.N., the General Secretary of the Peace Pledge Union, the Librarian of the Fawcett Library, and the Director of the Cambridgeshire and Isle of Ely Branch of the British Red Cross Society.

As regards letters between Rose Macaulay and her friends, a considerable number have been made available to me, and I hope that all those concerned will accept my warmest thanks. Here I must make special mention of Dr Arnold Toynbee who as Gilbert Murray's literary executor has allowed me to publish passages from the correspondence with Professor Murray, and also Mr John Murray who has permitted me to quote from the files of his publishing house. I am also very grateful to Mr John Bunting for lending me the extensive series of letters to his father Daniel George, Mr David Ley for approving quotations from correspondence relating to Spain and Portugal, and Mr Frank Swinnerton and Professor Blair Rouse of the University of Arkansas for their courteous help regarding the letters to Mr Swinnerton. For access to other letters I am grateful to the Literary Trustees of Walter de la Mare, the late Miss Margerie Venables Taylor, Mr Benjamin Glazebrook, Mrs Caroline Michel, and the Librarian of King's College, Cambridge, as well as to the Henry W. and Albert A. Berg Collection, the New York Public Library, and the Astor, Lenox and Tilden Foundations. Finally I must emphasise my gratitude to the late Father Hamilton Johnson for making possible the publication of Rose Macaulay's letters to him. Although they have already appeared in *Letters to a Friend* and *Last Letters to a Friend*, certain passages are of such importance that they are also included in the present book.

Sir Geoffrey Keynes let me study the originals of some of Rupert Brooke's letters, a kindness I much appreciated, and he agreed to the quotation of a hitherto unpublished passage in one of them. I would also like to thank Lord Sackville for allowing me to quote from a letter written by the late Lady Sackville to Miss Jean Macaulay. The quotations from George Macaulay's letters to Francis Jenkinson are made with the permission of the Syndics of Cambridge University Library.

Acknowledgement should also be made of permission to reprint certain published material: Mr John Lehmann has kindly

ACKNOWLEDGEMENTS

agreed to the inclusion of passages from *Coming to London*, and the tributes entitled 'The Pleasures of Knowing Rose Macaulay' are republished with the permission of the authors (or their heirs) and of *Encounter*.

Constance Babington Smith

PART I

Chrysalis

1881 – 1917

I

'ROSIE'

EMILIE ROSE MACAULAY was born on the first of August 1881 at Rugby, where her father was an assistant master at Rugby School. She was a second daughter, which to her mother, who had been hoping ardently for a son, was a sad disappointment. Possibly some echo of this vexation communicated itself to her baby: as a girl 'Rosie' was very much a tomboy, and for years she believed that she would one day grow up 'to be a man'. Later too, in her novels, Rose often gave names to her heroines which could equally well have been the names of men.

Her parents, George and Grace Macaulay, were cousins,[1] and among their ancestors and relatives were many clergy, as well as liberal-minded intellectuals and men of commerce, with here and there (on the side of Rose's mother, who was a Conybeare) an eccentric scholar. Her father, the eldest of a family of seven, was by nature studious and painstaking; he had been a scholar at Eton and also at Trinity College Cambridge. Kindliness and reserve were his outstanding qualities and he had a seriousness that tended towards melancholy. In sharp contrast Rose's mother was quick, vivacious and an amusing talker. She was also an egotist, for she was an only daughter and had been spoilt as a child. The Conybeares, who originally came from Devonshire, had even more links with the Church than the Macaulays, and Rose's mother was a devout High Church Anglican; before her marriage one of her keenest interests had been running a Sunday-school

---

[1] George's grandfather, the Rev. Aulay Macaulay, was a brother of Grace's great-grandmother Jean Babington. See Genealogy, p. 237.

class. By temperament Grace Macaulay was not scholarly – her opinions usually sprang from impulse and emotion – but she read widely and delighted in learned discussions.

A certain amount of information about Rose's early childhood can be gleaned from her mother's diaries, and although the entries are spasmodic and there are considerable gaps, they give us a lively picture of the home into which Rose was born, with its public-school rhythm and the leisurely coming and going of relatives. Through the eyes of the young Victorian wife we can follow the outings and the entertainments, the frequent church-going and almost equally frequent rows with the servants, the reading aloud, the stimulating conversations, and the round of family visits in the school holidays.

Rose's parents had married for love, and their happiness is reflected in many of the entries, such as the following, which was written by Grace in January 1879, shortly after she and George arrived at Rugby, fresh from their Italian honeymoon.

Rugby life delightful . . . George always rushing in from school in cap and gown. I am never lonely. Our drawing room is so beautiful and bright no one could help being happy in it; and all the other masters and their wives kind and neighbourly. We spend our evenings amid heaps of books by our warm fire and hearth of blue and white tiles. George reading me selections of Plato, Shelley, Pope, Swift, Dickens, Byron, Sophokles [sic] . . . or other Greek – scraps of Sappho etc.

After their reading she evidently retired first, for later in the term she wrote 'Why do I have to come down *every* night in dressing gown and slippers and wake George by main force (sometimes with wet sponge) from sleep over the fire?' In her happiness she could even jubilate over breakfast guests: 'We have boys to breakfast three days a week. Great fun sometimes.' In the afternoons there was the ritual of paying calls, and the chance to find congenial friends: one of the Rugby wives Grace saw most of, for she was almost a neighbour, was Rupert Brooke's mother, whose eldest son Dick was born in the same year as Rose. This was the beginning of a lasting friendship between the Brookes and the Macaulays.

For their first Easter holidays together the young Macaulays went first to stay in Shropshire with George's mother, who was a widow. She lived in the village of Hodnet, where her husband, a first cousin of Lord Macaulay, had been rector. Next they went on to Surrey to stay with Grace's mother at Weybridge. Mrs Conybeare, one of the Rose family, was like Mrs Macaulay a clergy widow,[1] a woman in whom wit and wisdom were combined with real goodness. For Rose, later on, she was to be a beloved and admired grandmother – in fact she was the only grandparent she ever knew, for Mrs Macaulay died in 1881. After Weybridge there was one more family visit. On their way back to Rugby the Macaulays paused briefly at Barrington near Cambridge, where Grace's only brother was vicar. Edward Conybeare, who had already been married for some years and had a growing family, was twelve years older than Grace and an affectionate but somewhat overpowering elder brother.

The Macaulays' first child, Margaret, was born in March 1880. Subsequently Grace suffered from poor health for some months, but by August she was well enough to enjoy a day in London with George en route for a summer holiday at Southsea and on the Isle of Wight.

We spent an hour among the . . . Greek sculptures in British Museum, discussing partly Ruskin's theory that all works of art not by a definitely religious man degenerate into 'mere lust of the eye' (whatever that may mean as distinguished from *all* delight in the beautiful). Among those old sculp-

[1] Her husband, the Rev. William John Conybeare, who had died of tuberculosis at the age of forty, had been the first Principal of the Liverpool Collegiate Institute and in his day a noted writer on ecclesiastical subjects.

tures, feeling their elevating refining influence so intensely, it seems too absurd a view to me.

During the holiday she reported other interesting conversations, one of them at Southsea with some Macaulay cousins.

In eve[ning] all sat out on balcony looking over the moonlit sea with distant strains from the band on the pier. Family talk over character etc. and the past Macaulay history – how the Macaulays harried the Morisons on the Isle of Lewis and in revenge the Morisons exterminated our ancestors all but one boy, foster-child to a Morison woman, who saved him, from whom we all spring.

On the Isle of Wight an adventurous new diversion for both Grace and George was riding a hired tricycle: 'I upset once going too fast down steep hill, which I shall not do again.' Soon they were keen to obtain a *double* tricycle, and when they went on to Weybridge George made a special trip to London to try and find one, without success. They had better luck after returning to Rugby. In nearby Coventry they bought a secondhand double tricycle for £12, and afterwards rode it home, a distance of about ten miles, in two and a half hours. All went well until they were almost back; then George took a hand off the handlebars to lift his hat to a friend, and they ran into the kerb, which made Grace cross, 'my purchases for baby having rolled into the road'. Unlike some of the masters and their wives, the Macaulays had no carriage, and it pleased them greatly to be able to explore the country near Rugby on their unusual machine. During that autumn their expeditions included one of seventeen miles and another of twenty-five.

The year 1880 was clouded for Grace by the death of one of her cousins, her mother's niece Emilie Rose. Emilie, who was four years older than Grace, and only twenty-nine when she died of cancer, had been a lovable and very pious person. Grace, as well as many others, had worshipped her. 'To me her influence for good can never be forgotten – softening womanly charity and humour to perfection.' It was very natural that when a second daughter was born to the Macaulays in the summer of 1881 she should be named after her.

Unfortunately Grace Macaulay's diaries for 1881 and 1882 are missing and we know hardly anything of the first year of Rose's life. One little sidelight occurs however in the journal that Edward Conybeare kept regularly for almost all of his life. Three weeks after the new baby's arrival he wrote 'To Rugby . . . Found Grace wondrous well, and *Emily Rose* very like me'. This is the only mention we have of a resemblance between Rose and her mother's side of the family (Grace Macaulay, a typical Conybeare, was dark with violet-blue eyes and a broad forehead) and allowances should be made for Uncle Edward's powers of imagination, which in the family were notorious. There is a more reliable record in Grace's diary for 1883. When Rose was eighteen months old,[1] so her mother noted, people were saying that she was very like her father – he was a good-looking man with fair curly hair and a thoughtful expression – and this is indeed obvious in contemporary photographs. Years later Rose referred to these early photographs of herself as showing 'a funny chubby little creature'. But more striking than the chubbiness is the flower-like look of the grave little face framed with luxuriant fair curls, and the air of slightly apprehensive wonder in the candid gaze.

By 1883 the nursery party consisted of three little girls; another daughter, Jean, had been born in 1882. But the Macaulays' fourth child was, to Grace's delight, a boy, and he was given the family name of Aulay. For the following two years the sequence of events cannot be followed in detail, since two more of Grace's diaries are missing, and Edward Conybeare made only one or two mentions of the family (in January 1884 he recorded that Grace was 'seeking her sixth nurse in the twelvemonth!'). But there is a letter written by Grace to Mrs Conybeare at about this

[1] It seems that she was not known as 'Rosie' until she was slightly older.

time which is of note as showing that Rose and the others were not, as Victorian children often were, isolated from their parents by nursery protocol – perhaps one reason why Grace lost so many nurses.

Yesterday I did a thing of which I know you would approve: put the big round bath in the play room with lots of salt water in it, and let Margaret and Rose splash there to their hearts' content for nearly half an hour. They *did* make a mess – we shut them in quite alone! Jeanie and Aulay had just a touch of cold which forbade the joy to them, but I took them to see Miss Bucknill's parrot instead. George is eager for their next bathe that he may turn on the hose through the back garden door upon them! Today I couldn't allow it, for they are going out to tea and their hair gets too wet. I am making them bathing caps.

This glimpse of the young parents with their children can be supplemented by the memories of Jean Macaulay who, looking back to her childhood, recalls how their mother used to show them picture-books before they went to bed. She believed that children should not learn to read until they were four, and considered it 'bad for the brain' to begin earlier. But Rose, who was always quick, insisted on learning to read before the appointed time. And it was shortly after this that she and Margaret composed a story called 'Gish and Goo', the adventures of two little girls; Jean remembers thinking it wonderful, but unfortunately cannot recollect anything further. The age of four was also the time when their mother explained to them about God, and taught them to say a simple prayer. All except Rose took this as a matter of course, but, according to family legend, when it came to her turn her response was 'I don't know that'.

Rose, so Jean recalls clearly, was 'the good one' of the family, the best tempered and the most unselfish. Margaret (their mother's favourite among the girls) was 'nervy', with a violent temper, and Jean remembers a nurse saying scoldingly to her 'Look at

Miss Rosie, how good she is'.[1] The characters of the three little
girls are evident in a photograph taken of them as bridesmaids in
1886, when they attended their father's sister Anne, 'Aunt
Nannie', at her marriage to her cousin Charles Smith. Clutching
their posies and obviously ill at ease in their elaborate knee-length
crinolines, Margaret looks petulant and Jean obstinate while Rose,
then four and a half, appears tremulous and gentle, anxious
almost to tears though determined to go through with the ordeal.
Slight and delicately lovely she is by far the prettiest of the three.

For Rose's parents the year 1886 was a time of much anxiety,
chiefly on account of Grace's health. Trouble began in the spring,
an intensely cold spring, when there was a severe epidemic of
whooping cough in Rugby. All five of the children – Margaret,
Rose, Jean, Aulay, and the new baby, Will – went down with it,
and Aulay, Grace's favourite child, was by far the worst stricken.
She herself nursed him day and night, and before long her own
health was undermined. 'Can't get strong', she wrote in June.
'Dr Simpson says he expected it after the long strain of nursing
last term and the steam kettle atmosphere.' Edward Conybeare,
when he visited Rugby, found both Grace and George 'cruelly
worn down'.
   Through the summer things were a little better. The Headmaster of Rugby (Dr Jex Blake) lent the Macaulays his carriage for
the holidays, and the coachman, who was devoted to children, took
them for many pleasant outings. Then in August, soon after Rose's
fifth birthday, the whole party went with Mrs Conybeare to
Malvern and Wales. But before autumn Grace was increasingly
poorly and found herself suffering from 'symptoms' and 'worse
symptoms'. These proved to be the early signs of a tubercular
infection of the throat, a matter of special alarm in view of the
fact that her father had died of this same disease. During the

[1] During her childhood Margaret suffered from chorea (St Vitus's dance)
and the involuntary movements and grimaces caused her much distress.

winter she was seriously ill. 'Tidings of Grace in constant haemorrhage' Edward Conybeare noted in February 1887.

We do not know just when it was that the tremendous decision was taken: Grace must go to live in a warm climate, which would mean that George would have to leave Rugby to accompany her, and the whole family would move abroad. But it must almost certainly have been some time during the early months of 1887, not long before the birth of the Macaulays' sixth child Eleanor, an unwanted baby. For George, who was now thirty-four, the uprooting was going to mean the sacrifice of his professional career at a moment when there might have been an important new development; he had recently been hopeful of securing an appointment at Cambridge, now that the ban on married dons had been lifted. It would also mean a financial pinch, for the family would have to live almost entirely on his and Grace's modest private resources, though he hoped to earn a little by free-lance translations of the classics.

In Italy, the country they planned to move to, they could doubtless live very cheaply, but they faced an utterly uncertain future. They were not even sure beforehand where they would live, though they had decided to settle somewhere near Genoa. 'We left our dear Rugby home this afternoon after our nine happy years in it', Grace wrote in mid-September. 'Children into every room for final farewells.' Jean confirms this detail of the departure, and also remembers that Rose and Margaret kissed the walls, which she thought rather silly.

The Macaulay party stayed at Weybridge for their final weeks in England. 'Found Grace looking sadly frail, but specially sweet', wrote Edward Conybeare, and added 'Children improved by shorter hair'. The decision to cut off the children's hair had been made in the interests of hygiene, but in fact not all of them were shorn. When it came to the turn of six-year-old Rosie, their mother could not bring herself to have the beautiful soft curls cropped off.

2

VARAZZE

ON ARRIVING at Genoa the Macaulay party installed themselves
at a lodging called the Hotel Smith, and leaving the six children
with Fanny the nurse and Charlotte the maid George and Grace
set off to look for a house. After a few days, on the advice of a
local railway official, they went to investigate Varazze, about
twenty miles west of Genoa on the rocky Ligurian coast. Set
above a sandy bay, Varazze is now an overcrowded seaside
resort, but in 1887 it was a simple provincial town, described in a
contemporary Baedeker as 'a busy shipbuilding place'. Rose
herself, long afterwards, wrote of it thus: 'The little town lying
between sea and hills had deep stone streets smelling of fish,
drains, and roasting coffee, and deep arches opened onto the
shore, where they dried and mended fishing-nets, made rope, or
built ships.'[1]

Rose's mother in her diary refers to the palatial house they
found in Varazze, but a surviving photograph and Jean Macaulay's
memories indicate that what they found was actually a flat,
though it was certainly a large one, consisting of the spacious
upper floors of a house near the centre of the town, not far from
the twelfth-century church of Sant Ambrogio. At the rear there
was a first-floor balcony facing towards the bay, and below it a
terrace planted with orange trees, 'very sunny and warm', while
indoors the splendid drawing-room had a painted ceiling. The
owner, Dr Carattini, agreed to let the apartment to them for a

[1] See 'Villa Macolai', R.M.'s contribution to *Little Innocents: Childhood
Reminiscences* (1932).

rent of six pounds a month, and two days later, on 29 October, the Macaulays moved in, accompanied by their domestics who now included an Italian maid-of-all-work, Teresina.

Thereafter Grace's diary glows even more than usual, despite a nursery epidemic of measles. Her own health is not even mentioned. 'Glorious sunny day . . . I spent the morning basking on sands with the well children . . . Up hills (George and I with Rosie) in the afternoon, finding fresh mountain paths and gathering wild heaths and berries. Our rooms full of wild flowers. Snow-topped mountains behind our nearer hills most beautiful.' Unpacking supplies from England was an operation she seems to have relished; as a semi-invalid she could only supervise. In mid-November she wrote:

Fifteen of our boxes and packing cases arrived . . . George opened and unpacked them in huge entrance hall and we got up contents chiefly by hampers let down with cords from the inner balcony in the middle square of the house. Fanny, Charlotte and the children too helped excellently. We found about twenty pots of jam smashed and the contents let out over the rest, so the 140 whole pots had all to be washed before we could put them away. A nail had run into a tin of carbolic acid also which saturated a lot of things, but we were all cheerful and worked all day with only cocoa and bread and butter to eat so as to waste no time. George quite overdone by midnight as he had also carried many heavy loads upstairs.

A fortnight later there was more unpacking. 'Our remaining boxes (all but one) came from custom house at Genoa today and we put our dear drawing-room and dining-room carpets down . . . and hung our own pictures and made the whole place beautiful and home like. Children wildly delighted.'

By the time the family had been in Varazze for about a month their life followed an established routine.

The order of our days is this: George rises at seven or so –

Margaret, Will and Aulay (who sleep in cots about our room)
at a little before eight. Rosie comes in to dress with Margaret
– boys to nursery. I dress with M and R near paraffin stove
except on very warm days. Breakfast (whole family but baby
[Eleanor] together) in dining room downstairs at 8.30 or so.
Then out on balcony opening out of dining-room. Then
(after an interval) I go shopping most days for household
supplies with children, who are given biscuits at shops; then
to lessons, Aulay reading; Jean reading, writing, needlework;
M and R Italian, writing, dictation, needlework. Then on
sands before the house enjoying ourselves till dinner 1.30.
After dinner George and I (G has worked at [his] Herodotus
[translation] all the morning) go off on a mountain climb or
other charming walk with a few children till 5 o'clock tea.
Then often to Benediction. Then children all together till
their bed time (I show pictures or read simple stories first,
then as the younger ones drop off to bed we go on to
Shakespeare which is Margaret's and Rosie's great joy). I
visit each child alone in bed for prayers or hymns and talk.
George and I get to our tea by 8.15 or so, and after that we
read together till bed time.

Such was the family's simple, regular life during their first
winter as Dr Carattini's tenants. When summer came there was
the added joy of bathing, and George, whose kindness to his
family was one of his most endearing traits, would sometimes
leave his work to escort the bathing party. 'George carries down
tent for me, and cork floats, on which first children and then I
delight to lie, enjoying ourselves out of our depth.'

Here one may ask how George himself was adjusting to the
new life. It was undoubtedly a time of continuing anxiety for
him on account of his wife's illness. Writing from Varazze to a
Cambridge friend, Francis Jenkinson, who had recently suffered
a bereavement, he said that he could faintly realise what it meant
'from the dread which sometimes comes to me of being left

alone'. It was also of course a period of frustration for him as regards his work, for although he enjoyed his translating, and had brought plenty of books from England, and although in Genoa there were libraries and also a few British residents with similar interests to his, he was in effect cut off from research facilities as well as from academic friends. According to Jean her father grew increasingly taciturn at this time and she later learnt that he had become convinced, with some reason, that he was a failure. When his thirty-sixth birthday was nearing the children wanted to plan little presents for him, but their mother, so Jean remembers, told them not to take any notice of their father's birthday, because it would only depress him.

Just a year after the move to Italy Grace gave birth to a seventh child, Gertrude, a lovely little girl, whose beauty was in acute contrast to the plainness of Eleanor, now at the toddler stage. As a small child poor Eleanor had a miserable time for not only did the elder children look down on her as a baby – they called themselves 'the five' and were inseparable playmates – but their mother more or less ignored her. Again and again in the diaries Grace refers to 'the five children', for example, 'We took all five children to Teatro Storico . . . to see juggling with knives, bottles etc.' This outing, incidentally, took place on a Sunday; Varazze Sundays were notably unlike Victorian Sundays in England. The festas of the local Church were days of bliss for the young Macaulays because of the processions, with their pageantry and chanting and incense and clanging bells. 'Beautiful procession along the narrow streets', wrote Grace on the feast of Corpus Christi 1889, 'with tapestries hanging out of every window and flowers showered down by children till the ground was bright.' The most elaborate festivities of all were in honour of Saint Catherine of Siena, the town's patron saint. 'Today . . . the great procession of Santa Caterina . . . Little St John the Baptist with refractory lamb and all the rest of the picturesqueness.'

Quite apart from the Varazze festas was the religious education which the children received from their mother. At this time she began giving them 'Prayer Book lessons' every Sunday, and taught them to learn the collects by heart. A stirring teacher, she kindled their imagination by picturing the Christian religion as a battle for the Good and the Right, in which they themselves had to play a part. To Rose and her brothers and sisters the idea of participating in such a battle seemed extremely exciting. Looking back to these lessons Rose once said that never had she been more inspired by a longing to be good and to please God.[1] But it should be mentioned that the lessons also included teachings on the after-life which to children were terrifying. Jean, for one, remained convinced throughout most of her life that she was destined for hell fire.

Ideas of romantic adventure permeated Rose's day-dreams at the age of eight, and they were amply fed by her voracious reading. *Masterman Ready*, *The Little Duke*, *Ivanhoe*, *Tanglewood Tales* – these were some of the favourites she raced through, often lying sprawled under the nursery table. Also at about eight Rose became an ardent hero-worshipper, thanks to Charlotte Yonge. She lost her heart to 'Guy' in *The Heir of Redclyffe*, and for a year or two would creep under the sofa and hide if his name was mentioned. But the books Rose read to herself were by no means the only ones which became part of her life at this age. Every evening the children would gather round while their father read aloud to them, and it was thus that they became familiar with nearly all Dickens and Scott, *Robinson Crusoe*, *Lorna Doone*, *The Three Musketeers* and *Tom Jones* (Rose later discovered that 'the more vulgar bits' in the latter had been omitted).

Another family tradition was the setting of 'exam papers' by the grown-ups on the subject of books that all the children had been reading. And since the early education which Rose shared

[1] *Letters to a Friend*, p. 340.

with her brothers and sisters was almost entirely non-competitive it is of special interest that after one of these 'exams' their mother jotted down the individual marks, so giving us the only record of its kind of Rose's intelligence as a child. The book in question was *The Pied Piper*, and not only the young Macaulays but also several of their first cousins, the young Conybeares in England, took part in the 'exam'. Margaret who was nine scored 240 marks, next came ten-year-old Alison Conybeare with 204, then Rose (eight) and Dorothea Conybeare (nine) with 203 apiece, while Jean and the two boys followed after.

Grace's diary for 1890 includes one or two further scraps of information about Rose's abilities (she was then nine). For example it appears that a certain Signorina Erminia tried for a time to teach her to play the guitar. But Rose, like the rest of her family, lacked a sense of music, and the guitar lessons seem to have petered out after only a few months. There is also some unexpected evidence concerning Rose's handwriting. Alongside locks of their hair the children had written their names, and Rose's hand – in later life hardly decipherable – was then one of the clearest and neatest of the family. In this same diary there are various little entries written by the children, including one by Rose, which is the earliest surviving specimen of her writing. 'Me and Margaret and Jeanie went to Genoa with mother. We went to the gardens, and saw the white peacock, and then we went to the church. When we were going back there was a man with airbaloons [*sic*], and we bought one.'

In Varazze the Macaulays were the only British residents, and during their first few years they kept very much to themselves. But in 1890 Grace became friends with a Signora Massari, and was introduced to the Sardis, one of the leading families of the town. Attended by George, and arrayed in her best ('my heavy imitation seal edged with brown fur almost weighing me down'), she made a formal call on the Sardis, and later, according to a

diary entry written by Margaret, she made another call taking
the children with her. It was not an entirely enjoyable visit: 'We
went to Signora Sardi's house, and they gave us some grapes . . .
They kissed us all and we didn't like it.'

The children were far happier with their own relations than
with strange Italians, and now that the family was thoroughly
settled in Varazze they quite often had visitors from England.
Mrs Conybeare came several times for longish periods, and a
cousin called Daisy Smith spent a month with them, when she
tried to teach the children to draw. The Macaulay uncles were
especially popular; all four were unmarried and all of them loved
children. There was Uncle Willy from Cambridge, the mathe-
matician of the family and a Fellow of King's (it was through an
introduction from him that Roger Fry came to stay at Varazze in
1891). Then there was Uncle Kenneth, who was in business in
Birmingham, and could rig a toy boat or persuade a miniature
cooking stove to function. Uncle Harry was the happy-go-lucky
one who could never settle in a job; he enchanted his young
nephews and nieces by his lively renderings of music-hall songs.
Very different in character was Uncle Regi, Rose's godfather,
who at thirty-two had become a partner in an important East
India company (Wallace & Co). Uncle Regi had a great sense of
fun, and was also exceedingly generous. 'All enjoying Regi,'
Grace wrote on the occasion of one of his visits. 'He lets all five
children romp with him endlessly, builds magnificent castles for
them with the 150 new bricks, plays "Snap" with them in the
evenings, and makes our afternoon hill walks more delightful
even than usual . . . He gave a five pound note to the five
eldest between them on Saturday evening.' The sixpence-a-week
pocket money that each of the children had from their father did
not go far, but their finances, of which he kept careful accounts,
were often restored by such lavish tips.

While at Varazze the children received one of Uncle Regi's
most exciting presents, a pony called Pinz. All of 'the five' took

turns on him, the girls side-saddle in long riding habits. Rose and Margaret were soon confident horsewomen, but Pinz was too strong for the younger ones, and sometimes took the bit between his teeth and ran away. Jean remembers being very scared but not daring to admit to it, for in their mother's eyes cowardice was one of the worst of sins. Their grandmother, too, insisted on courage, and after one of her stays she repeatedly told Alison and Dorothea Conybeare that when Rose, out on Pinz, had met a brigand, she had pricked up the pony and galloped off safely, *'and she wasn't frightened'*. Years afterwards Dorothea asked Rose if the tale had been true.[1] 'Of course not,' replied Rose, 'I was frightened to death!' Eventually, after Aulay had been thrown and his head badly cut, Pinz had to be disposed of.

During the first three years at Varazze, Grace visited England each summer for about a month (these trips were financed by Mrs Conybeare) taking with her one or two of the children, first Jean, then Margaret and Rose, and finally the two boys. George meantime remained in Italy. Grace's health was gradually improving though her throat still gave trouble and she often suffered from hoarseness. In the summer of 1890 however serious illness came to another member of the family. Grace returned from England with Aulay and Will to find George looking 'ghastly' and during the following weeks he very nearly died of typhoid fever and pneumonia. Four doctors were called in and two of his brothers hurried out to Italy. Grace nursed him and finally, after he had twice suffered relapses, broke down herself. Not until mid-autumn was life back to normal.

Already Grace had been longing to own a house in Varazze, and now that the drains at Dr Carattini's had proved dangerous to health it was imperative to move. Thanks to a gift of a thousand pounds from Mrs Conybeare, the Macaulays were able to buy an imposing villa at the eastern end of the town, and to equip it with

[1] Dorothea was the Conybeare cousin with whom R.M. remained closest friends throughout her life.

Rose aged three

Will (*above left*), Jean (*above*)
and (*left*) Margaret and Aulay
as children

a drainage system from England. In May 1891 they moved to the Villa Levante, or, as it was soon known locally, 'Villa Macolai'.

The house which became Rose's home when she was ten years old was square and red and almost, but not quite, as grand as the adjoining Villa Camogli. Alongside lay a walled garden, fragrant with orange and eucalyptus, and before it a terrace opened straight on to the beach through high wrought-iron gates. Behind the house, just across the single-track railway line to Genoa, the hillside rose steeply and a winding path led up it amid olives and rock pines.

For Rose and her brothers and sisters the chief delight of their new home was its proximity to the beach. As Jean has put it, 'the sea was our playground'. Rose herself wrote years later of 'the smooth, warm blue sea . . . tideless, waveless, swaying gently up and down the shore, with a little dragging whisper as of a soft wind in a forest. And, putting out on it, a Rob Roy canoe containing five children, three in the middle and one astride on each end. For thus, on a fine summer evening, the Macaulay family was used to embark on its daily nautical adventure to the jut of rocks half a mile up the shore. Arrived at these rocks, the crew would turn pirates, maroon one another, find islands and treasure, fight for life, fling one another into the sea, overturn the craft and sit on its backside, and finally voyage home as wet as it was possible to be. Whether they were clad in bathing-suits or in frocks and knickerbockers made no difference to the wetness, but some to the conscience, as they came in sight again of the red house on the shore.'[1]

These off-shore adventures were only one of the many joys of the Villa Levante days. Some of Rose's most nostalgic memories were of the hill walks, 'with my father telling us stories from Herodotus, Froissart, or the *Inferno* (we enjoyed those infernal circles), or my mother spinning entrancing tales out of her head;

[1] See 'Villa Macolai'.

of wandering in and out of dusky, incensy churches, in which my mother could not kneel without wishing that the notice *Vietato sputare* were more frequently observed, of hanging about the dark little shops, with their sacks of coloured beans, long wands of macaroni, and lovely plaster madonnas, saints and cattle; of (after such visits) hunting fleas over one's person in vain (only one of us [Jean] could catch these insects; it was her special gift), of chasing round garden or *orto* after fleeing rabbits, ducklings, goats or dogs, of sitting alone in an olive tree up the hill or in an ivy clump on the top of the *orto* wall, reading or writing . . . spinning one's private interminable tales of perilous and heroic adventure by land and sea, while the mule carts jingled along the shore road, and the fishermen hauled in their heavy nets with loud cries of expectation and hope, and the hot sweet tang of the hillside above mingled with that of the sea below.'[1]

To crown all this Rose was now discovering poetry. 'Poetry flowed into life with surges of exquisite excitement. Tennyson, Shelley, Browning, Swinburne . . . [I had been] given a complete Tennyson when I was eight, and a complete Shelley (illustrated) next year . . . Shelley is an intoxicant: I suppose it was round about my tenth birthday that I used to wade along the sea's edge chanting, in an orgy of self-pity . . .

A heavy weight of hours has chained and bowed
One too like thee, tameless and swift and proud.'[2]

In the midst of this idyllic existence a tragedy came suddenly to the Macaulays: in April 1892 Gertrude, by now three, quite unexpectedly developed meningitis, and died within a few days. It is hard to judge to what extent, at the time, the other children took in what had happened. But we know that soon after the funeral Margaret, Rose and Jean, along with their mother, were

[1] See 'Villa Macolai'.
[2] See 'The Free Run of the Shelves', *New Statesman and Nation*, 4 December 1948.

taken by Mrs Conybeare for a trip to Venice, and one may guess that the excitement of this expedition restored the children's normal exuberance. The shock of losing Gertrude was however very profound for their mother, and it had most unfortunate repercussions. Jean has clear memories of this. She took to treating Eleanor, her unwanted, ill-favoured child, with open cruelty, which particularly distressed Rose and Jean. Thenceforward began a vicious circle of 'naughtiness' on Eleanor's part and savage punishments from their mother. Rose, many years later, reflected with compassion (in a letter to Dorothea Conybeare) upon the plight of Eleanor as a child: 'She was divided by years from the rest of us, who were all, so to speak, in one gang. So she was rather lonely, and I think it was that which made her take to stealing things (I mean, jam from cupboards etc., nothing serious, though once or twice she did take money).'

Grace Macaulay was always an impulsive mother, and one result of this was that Jean, as a child, suffered from a nagging feeling of insecurity: 'You never knew whether she would praise you or blame you.' Their mother was often more severe, it seems, to Jean than to Rose or to Margaret. She never concealed the fact that she preferred certain members of the family to others. It is revealing that Rose and Jean invented a game called 'Families' in which both of them acted the part of a mother, with twelve or thirteen children apiece. Each of the 'children' had a definite personality, and the two 'mothers' compiled periodical 'Charm Lists', in which they graded their families in order of current preference.

At about the time of Gertrude's death an experiment in education for Margaret, Rose and Jean was tried but after about six months abandoned. The three little girls, then aged thirteen, twelve and eleven, were sent as day pupils to a local convent school. Jean remembers that they had to learn by heart page after page of history, geography and so on (in Italian of course) and critical discussions of any kind were taboo. The nun who gave them religious teaching would often look up to heaven, exclaiming *'Pazienza! Pazienza!'* as Margaret or Rose argued some point, and she was horrified when they brought a bible to school. Relations with their fellow pupils were also strained. 'The little heretics' were not allowed to pray with the young Italians who called the English girls 'Long Legs' because their skirts were considered too short (the 'summer costumes' worn by the three sisters in 1890, sketched by their mother in her diary, were sailor suits with skirts just below the knee).

In Rose's view, so she later wrote, the time at the convent school was 'rather boring'. 'We thought the nuns silly. I see now that they were merely actuated by the charming prudery peculiar to nuns. On the very few occasions when we joined in a school walk, the nun in charge, when men came in sight, would modestly turn down her eyes and say to her flock: *"Abbasso gli occhi."* I do not remember if the little Italians lowered their eyes, but the little English certainly did not.'[1]

Rose, at twelve, was reaching her tomboyish stage, and often took the lead in the escapades of 'the five'. And she not only behaved like a boy but boasted of what she would do when she was a man. She was determined that she was going to join the Navy, and Jean was to join the Army. Not only at Varazze but when all the family (except Eleanor) visited London in the summer of 1893, the Macaulay girls and boys shared in the same boisterous games. No wonder that Edward Conybeare described the party as 'overwhelming' when they descended on his quiet vicarage on their way to Cambridge to visit Uncle Willy. 'Tumultuous day', he wrote after they left. 'Whole Varazze huggermugger swarming in by dinner train till six, when they went on to King's, Rose and Aulay soaked by swamping from canoe.'

The following year George and Grace decided that the time

[1] See 'Villa Macolai'.

had come for a move. During their seven years abroad Grace's incipient tuberculosis had receded and almost disappeared; there is little doubt that George, for the sake of his work, wanted to bring his exile to an end (by now he was doing some editing of Middle English texts), and there was no doubt at all that the children needed more orthodox schooling. In the summer of 1894, shortly before Rose's thirteenth birthday, the Macaulays pulled up their Italian roots and made the journey back to England.

3

GROWING UP

'STARTLING NEWS of Macaulays having taken house at Oxford!' So wrote Edward Conybeare in his diary in August 1894. If he himself had been in his brother-in-law's shoes, returning to England and needing a home close to suitable schools and to good facilities for his own work, it would have been Cambridge without any question. But egocentric Uncle Edward could hardly have guessed the main reason for the Macaulays' decision: according to Jean their mother had insisted that she could not live in Cambridge because it was too close to her elder brother at Barrington. There were however important additional reasons for the choice of Oxford. The Oxford High School for Girls was at the time under a notable headmistress called Lucy Soulsby (whose aim was to train her girls in 'true religion, good manners, and sound learning, *in that order*'). Aulay and Will could go as day boys to Mr Lynam's preparatory school. And in the Bodleian there were manuscripts that George particularly wanted to investigate and edit. Before long he was, in fact, asked by the Clarendon Press to undertake a piece of work which kept him busy there for years, the editing of the complete works of William Gower, contemporary and friend of Chaucer.

For Rose and her brothers and sisters Oxford meant a first encounter with an alien world of convention and discipline. Out of school 'the five' were able to revert to their normal ways, playing in the street, taking their tortoises to church, and perpetrating practical jokes on the neighbours. But at school it seemed to them vital not to be different from the other children,

38

and Rose and her sisters became painfully self-conscious about clothes. This was before the days of school uniforms and their mother, for economy's sake, shopped in slummy south Oxford. There she bought them outfits made of brown corduroy, which was especially embarrassing to the three because at this period corduroy signified 'working class'. Jean has not forgotten the jeers of the Oxford urchins as they passed, and the shouts of 'Corduroy breeches!'.

At school 'Emily', as Rose was now called ('Rosie' was thought too childish for a girl of thirteen) was not especially outstanding; her work, as Jean puts it, was 'about average'. But we know that History was her best subject, which is not surprising since she adored Bertha Browne, the History mistress. We also know that her wide reading at home made her more knowledgeable, and more broadminded, than some of her classmates. Long afterwards she wrote to Dorothea Conybeare: 'I remember when I was in the Lower Fourth, at thirteen, that another little girl, Joy Poole, told me in a whisper that Charles II had *Mistresses. She* was shocked (though pleased too) but I wasn't either. I felt quite blasée about mistresses.'

By fourteen some of Rose's browsing in the family bookshelves was having a further effect. It was undermining the childish faith that had originally been stimulated by her mother's 'Prayer Book lessons' and later by a craze for Thomas à Kempis. When she was prepared for confirmation she was troubled by secret doubts, so she later admitted, because she had been reading John Stuart Mill. She would have liked to ask the parson who was preparing her whether, as she really could not believe everything she was supposed to, she ought to be confirmed at all.[1] But in an agony of shyness she could say nothing, and decided to submit to the ceremony to avoid fuss. Throughout

---

[1] The clergyman in question was the Rev. E. C. Dermer, Vicar of SS. Philip and James, Oxford, the church where the young Macaulays attended children's services, and also Sunday-school classes.

her teens Rose was afflicted by the most intense shyness. At school she clung to her sisters, and they to her, for they were almost equally shy, and with strange grown-ups they were all of them tongue-tied. Even C. L. Dodgson (Lewis Carroll) who taught Logic at the High School, where he was immensely popular with most of the girls, failed to melt the icy reserve of the Macaulay sisters when he was invited to meet them at home (he was a friend of their father's). 'We liked him,' says Jean, 'but we were so *terribly* shy that he never came again.'

The exclusiveness of Rose's devotion to her own family is clear from a fascinating fragment dating from her fourteenth year, a legal Will Form on which she inscribed forty-two 'bequests'. Among the 'beneficiaries' not a single person is mentioned except her parents, brothers, and sisters. The document also provides interesting evidence as to what were her most treasured belongings at this age; first on the list is 'My dog Fido' who was to go to Will – Rose and Will were specially close playmates. An unexpected item is 'All my dolls', to go to Eleanor. Rose had taken to playing with dolls unusually late but when she went to the High School her mother insisted that she must give them up; Eleanor, however, was only seven when the family moved to Oxford. Also on the list were a diamond ring, 'all my knives', a Venetian mirror, a swing, a stamp album, a moonstone brooch, a Burne-Jones picture, stilts, and wooden skates. The books which were specified by name were as follows: 'My Bible', *Hymns A & M with Tunes*, *John Gilpin*, *Devon Boys*, *History of Italy*, *Fur and Feathers*, *In the Golden Days*, and *Story after Story and Every Word True*.

At fourteen how did Rose look? A faded snapshot probably taken during her first year at the High School shows her gazing wistfully, even sadly, into the far distance. In another, taken perhaps a year or so later, she again appears grave and thoughtful. Like her mother Rose was gifted with an infectious gaiety, yet there was always in her a tendency to her father's pessimism. And from some doggerel verses she wrote in her mid-teens we can guess the main reason for her melancholy at this time – the move from Varazze had left her uprooted and profoundly nostalgic.

> Remember how the sun set, and lit the low sea,
> How smooth it was and purple, how wide, how free!
> How splashing waves slumbered at close of day,
> And the great sea was silent in one soft sway . . .
> Sweetly comes back to me, on a wind from long ago
> Breath of moon-bathed garden, where tall lilies grow;
> Oh, strangely comes back to me from pine-grown hill
> Sobbing of a nightingale – I think it sobs still . . .

Suburban Oxford was no substitute for Italy, but during the years there Rose and her family spent many happy holidays at the Worcestershire home of one of her uncles, Kenneth Macaulay. Clent, with its outdoor life and blissful freedom, was far more akin to Varazze, and more nearly home to 'the five', than Oxford could ever be. Cricket was a favourite game there, popular with girls and boys alike, and various young friends who lived nearby came and joined in the play, including the local squire's son Eddie Amphlett, who was secretly worshipped by Rose and also by Jean. The cricket field was one of the few places where the Macaulay sisters could forget their shyness. Rose, like her father, was naturally athletic, and she and the others, despite ankle-length skirts, bowled and batted and fielded with energy and skill. She also enjoyed the riding; Uncle Kenneth had several ponies and nearby, too, for a shilling or so, one could hire a 'Clent pony', and canter off over the hills.

Occasionally while Rose was in her teens there were jaunts to London, to stay with Mrs Conybeare at the house in Kensington that she rented every summer, and one of Rose's birthdays was celebrated by an expedition to the Crystal Palace to see the fireworks. There were also, during Rose's final years at school, one or two interludes further afield. Grace Macaulay still had to nurse her health, and twice she returned to Varazze for part of the winter, taking with her some of the children. Rose went both times, and after the first, when she was seventeen, she wrote some sombre verses entitled 'The Sea' which she entered for a school poetry competition. Her poem was published in the school magazine in December 1898 – it was easily the winner – and so far as we know this was the first time that one of Rose's compositions appeared in print.

On 29 July 1899, a few days before Rose's eighteenth birthday, so her mother noted in her book of anniversaries, 'Emily left school and put up her hair.' But although her hair was up, and she was officially no longer a child, she was still abnormally immature. In physical respects, so Jean remembers, she was an exceptionally late developer. She also seems to have lacked the impetus to try and get away from home, unlike Jean, who as soon as she left school at seventeen resolved to try and become a nurse. This idea of Jean's was regarded with vehement disapproval by her mother, who saw no reason why unmarried daughters should not be content to live at home. Thus Rose would almost certainly have continued living at home in north Oxford (like Margaret and Jean) keeping her mother company, feeding the poultry, and playing tennis and bridge, if it had not been for an unexpected piece of good fortune. Just before leaving school she had passed the Higher Certificate examination, with a distinction in History, so the way was open to a university education. But the expense was out of the question as far as her father was concerned, faced as he was with the boys' public-school fees (Aulay, who hoped to enter the Army, had gone to Clifton in 1897, and Will, the least intellectual of the family, to Marlborough in 1898). At this point however Rose's godfather Uncle Regi intervened with an offer to finance her three years at college. In the autumn of 1900 she came up to Somerville to read Modern History.

No letters or diaries from Rose's undergraduate days have

come to light but there are a few mentions of her in the magazine of the Oxford women's colleges, *The Fritillary*, and some of her contemporaries have had lasting memories of her. One of them has said that her complexion was 'just like a wild rose', another that when she came up she looked like an unfledged bird, 'shy and vulnerable', and that she was rather slovenly in her ways. Her hockey has been mentioned, as well as her fondness for boating, and her passion for climbing trees and roofs. All this is quite 'in character', but another thing which struck her Somerville friends represented, unknown to them, an extraordinary change in Rose. They found her affable and forthcoming, a chatterbox who gabbled away so fast that at times she was hardly intelligible, a ready speaker who made lively contributions to undergraduate debates. In the opinion of Jean, Rose's new ability to talk easily, which came to her when for the first time she had to stand on her own feet away from her family, was by far the most important effect of her time at the university.

Rose's years at Somerville ended with an academic fiasco. In 1903, instead of qualifying for a degree she was awarded an Aegrotat, which means that although, for reasons of health, she failed to complete her papers for the Final Honours examination, her tutor considered that if she had done so she would have deserved at least a good Second. An Aegrotat is thus a compliment to ability, for it shows that the authorities are not content to let the candidate be branded, by default, as 'Failed'.

The evidence as to what went wrong in Rose's case is inconclusive. According to Jean she had been down with influenza just before Schools, and when she tried to start the papers had to give up. Whereupon her father intervened with her tutor, and the Aegrotat award resulted. But one of Rose's closest friends at Somerville, Olive Willis, has referred to her 'refusal' to sit for the examination and says that the reasons were never explained. 'It may have been due to temporary ill-health but . . . more probably to a dislike of formal questions and answers when there seemed so much more to say on every subject.' Miss Willis has maintained that Rose herself took her failure very much to heart. Nevertheless it seems that she was able to enjoy herself, or at least to pretend to, during her final days at college. There was a going-down party at which every girl wore a costume representing her 'totem', i.e. the animal she was considered, by herself or her friends, to resemble most closely. Rose, so one of her friends, Lucie Savill, remembers, was disguised as a caterpillar: 'I see her in pale green from head to foot and with a small green headdress, most becoming.' It would be interesting to know who made this choice of costume. Perhaps Rose herself felt that as far as examinations were concerned she resembled nothing more than a despicable worm, but it is tempting to imagine that her friends, seeing her so green and abject, already sensed that a very different future lay ahead of her.

Another scrap of evidence indicating that Rose was able to make light of her failure is an amusing little sketch, drawn by herself, which she sent to one of her friends in the History School, Margerie Venables Taylor, soon after the results were out. Inspired by the croquet game in *Alice in Wonderland,* the sketch is captioned 'The Flamingo and the Hedgehogs: a Story of Schools'. It shows Miss Lees, Rose's tutor, in the guise of a flamingo, with two hedgehogs in play labelled 'M.V.T.' and 'E.R.M.'. The former, curled up obediently into a ball, is in position to be shot through a hoop, but 'E.R.M.' is hurrying cheerfully away from the hoop nearest to her. Yet in spite of the lightheartedness of this sketch Miss Taylor, many years later, made the following comment: 'E.R.M. rarely came to Somerville after she went down, and I have always wondered whether she could not face a kind of shame she felt at the Aegrotat.'

During the first year that Rose was at Somerville her home was still in Oxford. But in 1901 her father applied for a post as Professor of English Language and Literature at the University

College of Wales at Aberystwyth. Although he much preferred
working alone and at his own pace, the four volumes of Gower
had taken him more than six years and the work can hardly have
been lucrative. It seems that he had little choice but to return to
teaching. 'I have now to be prepared to teach almost anything –
much more than I know, at any rate, and I have to spend my
time in learning', he wrote to Francis Jenkinson when he had been
in Wales for a few months. 'We are living at a distance of four
miles or so from Aberystwyth, making it quite an adventure to
go in and out to my work – walking, driving [by pony trap],
cycling or by train. Our house is well sheltered by hills and
surrounded with woods, a very pretty place, and a paradise for
birds and probably also insects.'

Edward Conybeare, after his first sight of Ty-issa (The Lower
House) wrote of it in more effusive terms. 'An extraordinarily
out of the world but very pleasing abode in hillside clearing,
overhung . . . by dense woods . . . [with] a fairy woodland ravine
hard by' and 'a delicious green path through firs above the

45

house.' Rose's mother called Ty-issa 'our cottage', but it was capacious enough to take not only herself, George, Margaret and Jean, but Rose during her vacations, Aulay, Will and Eleanor (now at boarding school) in the holidays, a couple of maids, including at one stage an Italian cook, and also an occasional visitor or two.

It was taken for granted that Rose would live at home when she came down from Somerville in 1903, and thus began for her a three-year period of quiet country existence, punctuated only occasionally by visits to Clent or elsewhere (those to London were fewer now, for Mrs Conybeare had died). Each day began with family prayers, which according to Dorothea Conybeare were 'most painful musically... Aunt Grace played the piano very badly for the hymn, with lots of wrong notes – though she did have a sense of time. Uncle George joined in: there were three notes he could sing. One could not help thinking "Whatever can the Welsh maids think of the English 'music'?". The oddness of those Macaulay family prayers can hardly be exaggerated.'

Rose attended family prayers as a matter of course, but by now she made no secret of her agnostic doubts, which Somerville had done nothing to lessen. By her brothers and sisters it was regarded as a hilarious joke that in their mother's book of anniversaries, the quotation which happened to be allocated to Rose's birthday was a particularly pious one, and therefore laughably inappropriate:

> 'Tis religion that can give
> Sweetest pleasure while we live;
> 'Tis religion can supply
> Solid comfort when we die.

The days in the Welsh valley slipped by gently, highlighted only by the social doings that the Macaulays shared with the neighbouring English-speaking gentry, and also, but less often, with the families of the Aberystwyth dons. Grace Macaulay apparently enjoyed the leisurely routine and Margaret, to judge from a surviving diary, accepted it without question. Jean, on the other hand, chafed at the shallowness of the life, though she was able to escape to a certain extent by learning Welsh and mixing with the local peasants. Rose, perhaps even more than Jean, felt frustrated at having to live in rural Wales. The company of Margaret, of whom she was very fond, was some consolation, but she missed the intellectual stimulus of Somerville and became restless, argumentative and very critical, especially of her mother. On one glorious spring day, so Margaret wrote in her diary, 'Only Rose cavils at the weather, for being incongruous.' And then next day: 'Heavenly weather still, larch trees and primroses and gorse all smelling very sweet and strong . . . After tea . . . played an exciting game of croquet with Father, Rose helping with advice . . . when she had done disagreeing with Mother, up in the wood, about whether larch trees are nicest straight or crooked.'

Rose was far happier alone in the larch woods, as well as out on the cliffs, for then she could steep herself in the wild beauty, later trying to recapture it in the poetry that was her chief solace. By 1905 her verses were being published occasionally in the *Saturday Westminster Gazette*, which ran weekly poetry competitions. They were most of them romantic in flavour, such as the following, which she called 'Song of Prosper the Knight'.

> Sweet, like the smell of the wine in a fishing city,
> – (A small stone city, set round a blue-washed bay) –
> Keen, like the breath of the sea over wide peat-bog land,
> Young, like the odorous blowing of winds in May,
> Brave, like the birth of a poet's most high desiring,
> My lady Yvaine, sang Prosper, did pass this way.

But not all the verses she wrote at this time were so high-flown; a few were flippant and topical. 'Ballade of the Superior Person', for example, is an amusing jingle about the attitudes of a motoring 'expert' who had condescended to take some friends for a drive;

the refrain runs 'He's used, Sir, to a very different car.' Rose herself was already much enamoured of the automobile, though her normal means of transport was still a bicycle, on which she covered vast distances. Her enthusiasm for cars was certainly not shared by some of her elders. Uncle Kenneth hated them more and more, and Uncle Edward, after his first drive, noted solemnly 'Motoring more useful than pleasant.' Uncle Edward far preferred a bicycle. He was not only an ardent cyclist but also felt a personal affection for his machine, which he originally called 'Gerontius'. Later he renamed it 'Rosalind' because it had proved 'a very feminine creature, sensitive, responsive, wilful'.

Rose in her early twenties was still exceedingly young for her age. It was only when Aulay first appeared in Army uniform, as a Royal Engineer, that she was jolted out of the cherished dream that she herself would one day be able to join the Navy. But in spite of this disillusionment she was thrilled to have a soldier brother, as too were Margaret and Jean – they had all been caught up in the excitement of the Boer War. While Aulay was still at Woolwich Rose and Jean were invited to a dance there. We do not know whether Rose enjoyed it, but for Jean it was such an ordeal that she made a resolve (which she kept) that she would never go to another dance. Yet some of Aulay's friends had been favourably impressed by her, as well as by Rose, and afterwards told him, to his surprise, that he had pretty sisters. Margaret, who was also good-looking, but stately rather than pretty, was the one who went to dances most; their mother took her several times to Cambridge for the King's Ball. Rose, so far as we know, went only once.

Margaret was her mother's favourite companion and often accompanied her on visits, for example to Argyllshire, where Uncle Regi had taken an estate called Kirnan. She was also the daughter on whom their mother concentrated her matchmaking efforts. One of her fondest hopes, so Jean recalls, was to see

Views of the house and beach at Varazze

Rose in her twenties

George, Grace, Jean, Rose and Margaret (*l. to r.*)
at Shelford

Margaret engaged to Dick Brooke, Rupert's elder brother, a charming, delicate boy, who sometimes came to stay at Ty-issa. But in spite of much maternal scheming Dick did not become engaged to Margaret, or indeed to anyone else. When he was twenty-six he died after an attack of pneumonia. In retrospect one may question whether he would have been a 'suitable' husband. It is now known that the unfortunate Dick was an alcoholic.

By the end of 1905 the Macaulay family party was becoming much depleted. Jean had broken away at last, and was a probationer at Guy's Hospital. Aulay was serving in India. Will, whose practical bent and outdoor tastes had led him to an agricultural college, was soon to set off for Canada to farm – his departure would leave a sad gap, for he was by far the most cheerful of the family, with his loud laughter and schoolboy jokes. Eighteen-year-old Eleanor was now working towards a career as a teacher; her life away from home had been providentially transformed by the affection of one of the mistresses at her school, and she was now described by Uncle Edward as 'a dear, bright child'.

Rose and Margaret were the only two who were permanently at home with their parents, and the monotony of life at Ty-issa must have seemed all the more depressing to Rose after the excitement of a spring holiday in Italy, when she and Margaret, with Uncle Willy and Uncle Kenneth, stayed first in Naples and then in Rome. Such was the situation in which she felt moved to embark upon an entirely new venture. For the first time she would try her hand at a full-length novel. At about this same moment her father decided to apply for a Lectureship in English at Cambridge, and in December 1905 he was accepted. For Rose the prospect of liberation from the tedium of Wales seems to have served as a spur, for it was during the months before the move that she completed her novel, *The Aftermath* – she later renamed it *Abbots Verney* – and sent it to the London publisher John Murray, who was an Eton friend of her father's. Also during the earlier part of 1906 she became briefly involved in some voluntary social work, helping at a Settlement for factory girls in Chesterfield, where Olive Willis's sister was Warden.

As the summer wore on she was back at Ty-issa, and one day in July, when the move to Cambridge was nearing, and when (in Margaret's words) 'the hay [was] being cut in our field, and smelling very sweet', a letter came from John Murray to say that he would publish her book.

4

YOUNG NOVELIST

THE FLAVOUR of Rose's first book is utterly different from that
of the novels which made her famous twenty years later. *Abbots
Verney*, published when she was twenty-five, is a melancholy
story of moral failure and antagonism between the generations,
told with simplicity and in all seriousness. When Rose was well
established as a writer she tried to suppress it, as well as the other
novels she wrote before the First World War. She did not want to
be identified with books that she had come to regard as painfully
naive. But when *Abbots Verney* was published in December 1906,
and Rose's name first appeared in Murray's list alongside those of
well-known writers such as Edith Wharton and H. A. Vachell, it
had an excellent press and was called 'remarkable', 'singularly
clever', and 'a novel of great promise'. 'It is finely written,' said
one reviewer, 'the style is crisp, brilliant and pointed. There is not
a superfluous paragraph, line, or phrase. The book will make its
mark.' Family and friends were also enthusiastic. 'Original and
good writing', was Edward Conybeare's verdict, and Rose's
former headmistress Lucy Soulsby liked the book so much that she
wrote to John Murray 'I believe you have hit on a new writer
which I very seldom think when I read young women's novels!!
The feminist movement of the day does not conduce to a knowledge of human nature as it really is.'

Despite all this praise Rose's head was not in the least turned:
she was too keenly aware of the book's imperfections. In particular
she disagreed with the reviewer who thought there was not a

superfluous paragraph, line or phrase, and to her Somerville friend Margerie Taylor she declared that she ought to have made many cuts. 'I suppose it was such fun writing it that I went on and on and couldn't bear to condense . . . I should think each book one writes one learns a little more how to leave out, and select . . . The reviews amuse me immensely . . . Altogether the whole business is beyond words funny; if you want to be really interested and entertained publish a novel; it's quite worth it!'

She then went on to anticipate, with some apprehension, the reactions of the Somerville dons (Margerie was still working at Oxford).

I fear me the S[enior] C[ommon] R[oom] may be shocked at my having rushed into a printed book – I simply couldn't face them . . . I don't fancy it circulating in college, somehow; it's too trivial and unacademic to be smiled on there, and also it's too private-sentimental, serious, I don't know what – for me to like the idea of people I know reading it; I never can get used to it, somehow, it makes me feel so shy. However of course that can't be helped. It was to have been anonymous, you know, but Murray said it would be better not – sell better, he no doubt meant, and I suppose he's right. I'm glad you liked the Epilogue; at first there wasn't no Epilogue at all, but Murray said the end was 'too sombre', and demanded 'a gleam of light', and even particularized his gleam into an engagement; so imagine me sitting down with set teeth to manufacture it for him. I made it as vague and indefinite a gleam as I decently could, and sent it to him saying Will this do? Luckily it would, which I never expected; so in it went. But it isn't true, in its hints at engagements, though the rest is all right, I suppose. Publishers of course have you altogether in their grip; if they say you must do a thing you jolly well have got to do it. When he's paid himself what he spent on the book (if he succeeds in doing so) I get half the profits, if there are any, which there very probably won't be . . . anyhow I shan't know about all that till June, when they do their accounts . . . Of course I'm very interested in the question; I want both to earn a little money and keep Mr Murray in a sweet temper, against another time. Meanwhile of course it's a fearfully amusing occupation – so amusing that the financial side of it seems of very minor importance, except as a sort of a justification, to turn it from play to earnest; because I suppose one should be earning one's salt more or less. I don't earn mine, except when I extract an occasional guinea or two out of the *Westminster Gazette.*

This letter was written from Great Shelford, the village four miles outside Cambridge where the Macaulays had bought a house, Southernwood, and Rose added some scathing remarks about the surroundings of her new home. Although she had pined to escape from Wales, she was finding the flatness of Cambridgeshire distressingly dull. 'But why complain? There are at least three mountains in our neighbourhood quite six feet high [the Gogmagog Hills], so we ought to be contented. The natives regard them as young Alps. We mistook them for mole-hills at first: we have to be very guarded in our language on the subject when we converse with the inhabitants.'

Rose's second novel, *The Furnace,* was published towards the end of 1907. It was a shorter, subtler book than *Abbots Verney,* centring round a pair of shiftless adolescents, a twin brother and sister living in the slums of Naples.[1] It received less acclaim than her first book, yet when it had been out only a fortnight she was approached by another publisher who was eager for an option on her next novel. She felt however that she would prefer to stay

[1] Set entirely in Italy, *The Furnace* is notable as reflecting R.M.'s persistent nostalgia for Varazze, while the close companionship of the ingenuous 'Betty' and 'Tom' echoes the childhood camaraderie of R.M. and her brothers and sisters.

with Murray, though she was doubtful whether he wanted to keep her. 'Most certainly I should like to see your next novel', Murray replied to her timid inquiry. 'As you know, I do not rate *The Furnace* quite so high as its predecessor . . . but I hope that number three will more than carry out the promise of *Abbots Verney* . . . I have all along felt confident that you and your public will discover each other. *Abbots Verney* did very well for a first book, and I made every endeavour to call the attention of influential people to it.' He was working hard for *The Furnace* too, angling for American publication, and presenting copies of it to celebrities. When the Archbishop of Canterbury (Randall Davidson) asked him to recommend some good light reading he sent him *The Furnace* and *Abbots Verney* too.

Rose's 'number three', when it came, proved to be in quite a different style from her first two books. *The Secret River*, although in the form of a novel, was mainly an expression of her poetic impulse as well as a reflection of her recent reading, which ranged from Plato and Thomas Browne to Yeats and Maeterlinck. 'All picturesque Platonism, brilliantly clever', was Edward Conybeare's summing up. He liked the book so much that he read the whole of it aloud to his wife at one sitting. But neither Uncle Edward's appreciation nor even the favourable opinions of some of the reviewers can have meant much to Rose, because shortly before the book was published a family tragedy occurred which extinguished for her, as it did for all the Macaulays, the capacity for normal enjoyment. On 11 February 1909 Aulay, then serving on the North West Frontier, was murdered by native robbers. The impact of the terrible news on all of the family can be well imagined. A month later, so Edward Conybeare noted, Grace was still 'utterly stricken' and George 'quenched', while three months after the murder Rose remained 'sadly broken'.

Shock and grief for a while almost paralysed Rose, but at the same time a profound change of heart began gradually to come about in her. The confidence in agnostic theories which had taken hold of her in her teens seems to have dropped away under the stress of emotional crisis. Soon she was groping towards some sort of religious faith; during the next few years she became a dedicated believer. But for quite a time after Aulay's death there was no overcoming the numbness and anguish. Writing to Margerie Taylor in June 1909 she described her state of mind as follows:

> One of the minor troubles of a thing like [this] . . . is that it seems to take all the object out of life, and makes it difficult to feel it worth while to do anything of any sort . . . I have come to the conclusion that my besetting sin is Accidie – do you know Paget's sermon on it?[1] Consequently I sit at home and feel like a toad under a stone. I'm afraid I don't do anything these days, which is very feeble. I don't even write books . . . It is some time since I came up to Oxford, and I find the longer one stays away the less likely one is to come at all – it needs more pulling of oneself together than I feel capable of . . . I am so stodgy these days. I haven't an idea in my head or a word to bestow on anyone – total vacuousness and inertia . . . but that again is Accidie, I feel sure, and should be discouraged.

The horror of Aulay's murder still darkened Rose's outlook during the following year, when eventually she started on a new book. Her fourth novel *The Valley Captives* is by far the gloomiest she ever wrote; its recurrent themes are cruelty and failed human relationships. The reader's report (written by a friend of John Murray's, Lady Robert Cecil) emphasised that 'people who do not like being depressed will not be attracted'. Nevertheless Murray was clearly prepared to take trouble about Rose and he wrote gently to her, enclosing a copy of the report. He asked her to consider acting on various suggestions in it, but only if she found them agreeable. 'I never recommend but only suggest such change.' Rose did not take offence. She knew that the book

[1] Included in Francis Paget's *The Spirit of Discipline* (1891).

needed improving and asked humbly for further advice. Murray, much impressed, wrote to Lady Robert 'She deserves help because she takes criticism in the proper spirit ... I take a great interest in Miss Macaulay, and believe she will do a really good book some day, but she wants guiding.'

After Rose had revised her book Murray made a definite offer (a royalty of $12\frac{1}{2}\%$ on the first thousand of the 6/- edition, with 15% thereafter, and an advance of £50) but she still felt uneasy as to the book's prospects and her apprehensions were justified. When *The Valley Captives* was published in 1911 the critics condemned it as gloomy and grim and the sales were very disappointing. Rose took this failure much to heart, and after her first royalty statement arrived an interesting exchange of letters took place between herself and her publisher. 'I have just been looking at the accounts for *The Valley Captives* up to June 30th', she wrote, 'and I am afraid the royalties I ought to have received do not amount nearly to £50; so I am enclosing a cheque for £18 ... I am sorry it has not sold better, but I always felt doubtful about it.' To this Murray replied:

Dear Miss Macaulay,

I am very much gratified by your most kind and considerate note: all the more so because I think it is the first of the kind which I have ever received.

A practice has grown up of late years, by which a publisher pays, on publication, a sum in anticipation of royalties on a novel, but if the royalties do not reach that sum, he does not look for repayment, as he has taken the risk.

Last year I paid a very large sum to a well known 'lady' writer of fiction: her work was an inferior one when it came in: it did not succeed, and I lost heavily by it. I had paid this large sum before seeing the manuscript (a thing I very rarely do) as I heard she was hard up. When the work failed she turned on me and wrote me the most insulting letters, accusing me of being the cause of the failure!

I mention this to show you how much pleasure a letter like yours can give.

I return your cheque with very many thanks.

The Valley Captives, though commercially unsuccessful, marked an important new stage in Rose's career; it was the first of her books to appear in America. Henry Holt of New York agreed to issue a very small edition. And although Holt himself, after reading the manuscript, had told John Murray that the book's merit was 'terribly obscured and impeded by repetition, turgidity and splurge', it was widely reviewed throughout the United States, and thus for the first time the name of Rose Macaulay was brought before the American public.

Views and Vagabonds, Rose's next novel, was her earliest experiment in satire. It was a skit on what John Murray's reader called 'the fashionable cult for socialism and "the poor" '. Once more it was a story of failure, the failure of an idealistic young man to live out his principles effectively. 'I hope it will sell better than the last one', Rose wrote to Murray. 'It is certainly . . . more cheerful, if that helps.' *Views and Vagabonds* did sell considerably better than *The Valley Captives* and it had some favourable reviews; the *Spectator* called it 'a curious, clever book . . . a vivid, if somewhat fantastic sketch of the difficulties which confront our young intellectuals when they are involved in the intricacies of practice.' In America, Holt again published a small edition, but they only accepted the book after some hesitation because, as they pointed out with disgust to Murray, it was notably lacking in love interest.

In the meantime Rose was completing her sixth novel *The Lee Shore*, in which she reverted to her normal 'serious' style. Like all her books to date it was a story of failure. But this time she looked steadily beyond failure itself to what she called 'the gaiety of the saints'. 'Not the pleasant cheerfulness of . . . [those] who have things, but the gaiety, in the teeth of circumstances, of St

Francis and his paupers . . . the gaiety that plays the fool . . . that loses and laughs and makes others laugh in the last ditch; the gaiety of those who drop all cargoes, fortune and good name and love . . . and still spread sail . . . and when they're driven by the winds at last on to a lee shore, derelicts clinging to a broken wreck, find on the shore coloured shells to play with and still are gay.'

When she had finished the book Rose made a bold decision. She would not submit it at once to John Murray, but instead would enter it for a competition for novels that was being organised by Hodder & Stoughton, with prize money amounting to a thousand pounds (the first prize was for £600 and the second for £400). To her amazement *The Lee Shore* won first prize.

On 31 July 1912, when Murray saw the headline YOUNG LADY NOVELIST WINS £1,000 PRIZE, and learnt that the young lady in question was a cherished author of his own, his feelings were understandably mixed. But he wrote immediately to congratulate her.

Dear Miss Macaulay,

I have read in the newspapers today with sincere interest and pleasure that you are the winner of a large novel prize. I have always felt sure that you would 'come [in]to your own' some day and hoped that I might be associated with the event – but it has come in another and unexpected manner and will arrest public attention in a way which no reviews and advertisements can accomplish. Literary merit alone, unfortunately, cannot ensure success in these days, or you would have had your full recognition ere this. I trust that it is now assured to you. If at any future time there should occur an opportunity of our being again associated on some book it would give much pleasure to your sincere well-wisher

John Murray

In her reply Rose admitted that she found the award 'most exciting' and that she was 'of course very delighted to have got so much money all at once'. But she was as diffident as ever about the quality of her work. 'The book isn't a very good one, as a matter of fact, but fortunately the taste of the judges can't be very good either, so all was well. Perhaps it may make my future books sell better than the past ones – Hodder and Stoughton seemed to think it probably would, so I hope it will. Though I don't believe my books ever will sell really well. The results of this competition surprised me very much. I sent in mine because I thought it was more fun to, but I never thought it had a chance, and was contemplating approaching you with it in the autumn after I got it back rejected!'

Despite the triumphant début of *The Lee Shore* it was not a book to everyone's taste. Uncle Edward noted that some cousins at Weybridge with whom he discussed it were 'much down on *The Lee Shore*'. And although he gave copies of it to all his family, his own curt comment, 'A sad story', suggests that he failed to enjoy the paradoxical contrast between the success of its reception and its theme of failure.

The idea of rejection, loss, failure, of being at odds with society, had been dominant in all the novels Rose had so far written. Is it possible to discover the reason for this? Her Somerville friend Olive Willis later attributed it, at least in the case of *Abbots Verney*, to a continuing sense of shame at having gone down with an Aegrotat. That may well be part of the answer, but there may also have been a motivation with deeper roots, namely Rose's loyalty to her father. She adored her father, but in the family it was recognised that he was professionally a failure – he himself admitted it without hesitation. Thus it may be that Rose was striving in her novels, quite unconsciously, to convince herself that her father's failure by worldly standards was of no importance. For there were other values, personal relationships and personal integrity, which counted for so much more. In book after book she showed her sympathy for the feeble, the rejected, the despised, the outcasts, and it is notable that one reviewer of *The Lee Shore* praised her for her 'sympathetic treatment of unsuccess' and her 'tender handling of ineffectual lives'.

5

THE GOLDEN AGE

LOOKING BACK to the years just before 1914 Rose once called them 'that Golden Age', and she readily admitted that they were coloured for her by her memories of Rupert Brooke. She had known him quite well as an undergraduate, but it was after he established himself at Grantchester in 1909 that their friendship really began. In the perspective of her whole life it was an important friendship, chiefly because Rupert introduced her to literary London. His was the initial influence which caused the axis of her life, previously centred on family and home, to start gradually to shift towards independence. But besides this, and although there is no evidence of anything more than an easy companionship between them, it seems that she was, for a time, a little in love with him. In her book *The Secret River*, which she wrote in 1908, when Rupert was twenty-one, and she twenty-seven, the hero is a young poet just turned twenty. It may well have been as early as this that she came under the spell of his radiantly attractive personality.

As a family friend he had often been at Southernwood in his undergraduate days (especially during his first year, after the death of his brother Dick) for Sunday lunch, or for tennis, or for boating on the river. But at that time, so we can judge from allusions in his letters to his mother, he regarded Rose, as well as her parents and Margaret, with a certain amount of awe, though he appreciated the family's kindness to him and was fond of them too. Early in 1909, on hearing of Aulay's murder, he wrote to break the news to his mother and ended as follows: 'I don't

61

want to worry them or harass Mrs Macaulay, but don't you think I might write, to Margaret or Rose, at least? Because I should like to. They were very kind to me two years ago this term [at the time of Dick's death].'

After Rupert took rooms at Grantchester, to read for a Fellowship at King's, his relations with Rose became less formal and more spontaneous. The difference in years does not seem to have counted for much, perhaps chiefly because Rose was so young for her age. Poetry was, of course, a major bond between them. And as poets they were, in a sense, almost exact contemporaries, for their verses had first appeared in the *Saturday Westminster* at about the same time. Rose was never within the circle of Rupert's friends who congregated at the Orchard and later at the Old Vicarage. But we know that the two sometimes wandered together through the Grantchester meadows, talking meanwhile of poetry and poets.[1] Long afterwards, too, she recalled that they used to bathe together in the river.[2] And in *Views and Vagabonds* there is a description of two friends going off to Grantchester by boat: 'They rowed up a slow, weedy river, between foaming billows of meadowsweet, and landed and bathed beneath a weir, and lay in a field, and had a large tea, with muffins, at the Orchard.'

Rupert did not succeed in converting Rose to some of his ways of thought. In her newly religious frame of mind (to which we shall return in the next chapter) she was not at all in sympathy with his militant agnosticism, nor was she able to share his keenness for the Fabian cause. Reading between the lines of *Views and Vagabonds*, which she wrote impulsively in the summer of 1911, having temporarily set aside *The Lee Shore* less than half finished, one becomes aware that her feelings towards Rupert were at this time conflicting. The book which was her first satirical novel is full of echoes of him but its central theme is the

[1] R.M. to Walter de la Mare, 23 April 1915.
[2] R.M. to Father Johnson, 25 September 1952.

62

futility of blind allegiance to the Socialist ideal. It seems that when she wrote it she was coming to feel that she had had enough of Rupert's partisan eloquence; satire provided an easy means of redress. Even the title conceals a sly dig. One of Rupert's theories was that 'vagabonds of the spirit' were much more interesting than 'vagabonds of the body', while Rose regarded as the only worthwhile vagabonds those whose freedom was expressed, in the Varazze manner, by their overall behaviour rather than merely by talk.

There is also an interesting passage in *Views and Vagabonds* which directly mirrors her friendship with Rupert. In the summer of 1910 he had toured the New Forest by horse-drawn caravan, campaigning for Fabianism with his friend Dudley Ward. And at somewhere about this time (according to the memory of one of Rose's Shelford friends, Gladys Fanshawe[1]) he invited Rose to accompany him on a caravan expedition, 'a sort of camping holiday'. But the invitation had to be declined, to Rose's intense disappointment. Her father frowned sternly on the idea of a caravan holiday *à deux*, and although by now she was nearly thirty she accepted the paternal veto. In *Views and Vagabonds*, however, there is a chapter entitled 'The Conscientious Bohemian' which begins as follows: 'One understands that it is rather *outré* to travel alone with a cousin of the opposite sex in a van, even with the most fraternal feelings. Whoever lays down the law on these and similar principles of conduct would appear to have laid that one quite firmly. Of course the sensible plan is tranquilly to ignore the law, if one wishes to do so; the best people always do that with laws.' The quietly defiant tone of this last remark suggests that her father's ban continued to rankle for some time. In real life she had bowed to it, but in her fiction she could show her characters behaving just as they pleased, and she doubtless enjoyed portraying 'Cecil', the girl cousin of her hero 'Benjie', slipping off with him in a caravan unknown to her family. Then,

[1] Now Mrs Donald Macaulay.

in the story, comes a fascinating twist. When bedtime arrives on the first evening the two cousins part company; the girl goes off to a room in the local pub while the young man spends the night in the caravan. Here Rose seems to be saying to her father, 'You see, I can be trusted. You could have let me go.' But the manner in which she describes the little incident, the touching naiveté of her wording, speaks in moving fashion of the innocence of her outlook at twenty-nine. 'I expect you'd better go up to the inn about now', says Benjie at 9.00 p.m. ' "We've got to make a good impression on the village." Cecil was going to sleep at the inn. It was rather dull, but more correct.'

Nearly half a century later Rose, in her seventies, looked back to her 'Golden Age' and pondered over the changes that had come about in the 'social relationships of men and women'. 'Yes', she wrote to a friend,[1] 'I'm sure [they] . . . have changed a lot. Not that I . . . didn't go about quite freely with young men on walking tours, bicycling, bathing together, days out, games (hockey and tennis) river etc. etc. . . . Yes . . . friendships and outings with young men were common form. What *has* increased out of all knowledge is the further intimacies, which we (in my generation and class) never even conceived of, so far as I know. We should have thought such a notion excessively "low".'[2]

Grantchester was not the only setting for Rose's meetings with Rupert. She was also seeing him in London, and through him she made new friendships and acquired new tastes which were to become more and more an integral part of her life. Her memories of lunching with him in Soho were enduring ones, and she described them long afterwards in an essay entitled 'Coming to London.'[3] Rupert's friends, 'who were apt to be poets', such as

[1] Father Johnson.   [2] *Last Letters to a Friend*, pp. 32–3.
[3] It was one of a series by various contributors which first appeared in the *London Magazine*. Subsequently these essays, edited by John Lehmann, were published in book form as *Coming to London* (1957).

Edward Thomas, Wilfred Gibson and Ralph Hodgson, sometimes came to lunch too, usually at the Moulin d'Or. 'I was envious of Rupert, who walked about the streets without a map, often with a plaid rug over his shoulders, as if he were Tennyson, which seemed to me a very good idea and gave him prestige, and people turned to look at him as he strolled through Soho with his golden hair and his rug, and I was proud to be with him.' With Rupert, too, she first saw the Russian Ballet; Pavlova in *The Swan*, Nijinsky in *Spectre de la Rose*. 'We went ballet mad . . . It was, to those who hadn't seen ballet before, a new kind of aesthetic enjoyment, and intoxicating.'

Not for long however did Rose have to depend on Rupert for her links with London. Through her connection with the *Saturday Westminster* she met Naomi Royde-Smith, who was then, in her thirties, making a conspicuous success of the paper's 'Problems and Prizes Page'. This meeting with Naomi was a crucial event in Rose's life, for 'Miss Royde-Smith' took a fancy to her and before long adopted her as a protégée. Meanwhile Rose on her side had been swept off her feet, dazzled by Naomi's looks but even more by her mind and her conversation. Fair-haired, petite and attractive, with a liking for stylish clothes – her friends remember her furs and her dangling ear-rings – Naomi was a sparkling talker, though she was at times malicious and could also be very crushing. As a hostess she had already won quite a name for her parties, informal evening gatherings when she held court among her well-known friends – most of them writers – and took pleasure in introducing young newcomers. Rose with her flow of chatter and her gift for repartee was just the kind of promising young author Naomi liked to cultivate. And there is no doubt that Rose herself enjoyed these occasions – as all her life she enjoyed parties – though the vividness with which she later described, in *Crewe Train*, the emotions of an unsophisticated young woman plunged into a set rather similar to Naomi's suggests that she felt, anyway at first, uneasy and gauche.

Not only at these evening parties, but over lunches in little Fleet Street restaurants, Rose became gradually familiar with Naomi's circle of friends. At its centre was Walter de la Mare, then nearly forty and Naomi's devoted admirer, while others within it were J. C. Squire of the *New Statesman*, William Beveridge, then in his early thirties and working at the Board of Trade, Hugh Walpole, 'rosy with success and very cheerful and pleasant and friendly,' Middleton Murry, creator of the quarterly *Rhythm*, who was then reviewing for the *Westminster* and had just embarked on his affair with Katherine Mansfield. '[They] seemed to me, an innocent from the Cam', Rose declared in 'Coming to London,' 'to be more sparklingly alive than any in my home world . . . I liked them all. They were all gay and intelligent and young or youngish, and haloed to me with the glamour and sophistication of Londoners; they chattered of the literary and political world and its personalities as initiates – or so it seemed to me, who was a Cambridge provincial. These people seemed to me to be the people I felt at home with and liked to know, and I wished that I too lived in London.'

Amidst all this talent and charm Rose found Walter de la Mare the most delightful of all. 'He was very beautiful, and had a fantastic wit and funniness . . . I never, by the way, heard him called Walter, but always W.J. or Jack . . . He was a fascinating and fantasy-chasing conversationalist, and I fell deeply in love with him and with Naomi Royde-Smith. He and she with her gay and ridiculous wit and her wide literary range and critical appreciation, fitted exactly together.' De la Mare's poetry, too, enchanted Rose, though apparently she did not like the way he read it. At the Poetry Bookshop, where new poetry was not only sold but read aloud, she heard him reading some of his works, and had to admit that he did so deplorably (though we do not know just why she found his manner jarring). She much preferred the style adopted by Rupert Brooke, who read his poetry 'like poetry, not prose . . . He cadenced the lines, and made the rhythm apparent.'

In 1912 Rose saw little of Rupert, who was often abroad, though before he left for America in 1913 she was in touch with him again, when he was staying at Edward Marsh's flat in Gray's Inn. Not long after this she herself acquired a London pied-à-terre when Uncle Regi, generous as ever, enabled her to rent a small flat off Chancery Lane. This meant that she no longer had to ask Naomi or Uncle Regi to put her up when she wanted to stay in London, and that for the first time in her life, at thirty-two, she had a home of her own. Soon she took to spending several days of each week at number 19 Southampton Buildings, and parts of her new novel, *The Making of a Bigot*, were almost certainly written there.

The Making of a Bigot, which was published early in 1914 (it was Rose's second novel for Hodder and Stoughton) was described by Edward Marsh, in one of his letters to Rupert Brooke, as 'very clever and amusing'. But beneath the gaiety and the cleverness lay a serious theme, the crisis of conscience occasioned by a clash between loyalty to conventional ethics and the impulses of a warm heart. When Rose wrote it she was herself face to face with precisely the same conflict – not in her own life but in her attitude towards her new friends – since in Naomi's set sexual licence was on the whole accepted as a matter of course.

This novel was not Rose's only book to appear in the spring of 1914. Her first book of poetry, *The Two Blind Countries*, was published in May by Sidgwick and Jackson (who had also, three years earlier, published Rupert's first book). This collection of thirty-three poems, many from the *Westminster Gazette*, received some favourable notices. But it would not be justifiable to claim that it won a place for Rose among the recognised English poets of the day. Her poetry was never successful in the sense that her novels were. Yet for her it was a joy and a fulfilment, and for those who wish to understand her it is an invaluable reflection of some of her deepest emotions.

The pervasive impression left by *The Two Blind Countries* is one of sadness, isolation, and a bewildered groping; time and again the imagery reverts to greyness and mist, as in the final stanza of 'The Alien':

> On either side of a gray barrier
> The two blind countries lie;
> But he knew not which held him prisoner,
> Nor yet know I.

Some of the verses written after Aulay's death are predictably burdened with an awareness of human hate and spite. But others hint at a less clearly defined malevolence, at sinister, mysteriously brooding influences that Rose interpreted in the form of evil powers lurking in the fens and countryside near Cambridge. This is notably so in 'Trinity Sunday', one of the best known of Rose's poems.

> As I walked in Petty Cury on Trinity Day,
>   While the cuckoos in the fields did shout,
> Right through the city stole the breath of the may,
>   And the scarlet doctors all about
>
> Lifted up their heads to snuff at the breeze,
>   And forgot they were bound for Great St Mary's
> To listen to a sermon from the Master of Caius,
>   And 'How balmy', they said, 'the air is!'
>
> And balmy it was; and the sweet bells rocking
>   Shook it till it rent in two
> And fell, a torn veil; and like maniacs mocking
>   The wild things from without peered through.
>
> Wild wet things that swam in King's Parade
>   The days it was a marshy fen,

Through the rent veil they did sprawl and wade
  Blind bog-beasts and Ugrian men.

And the city was not. (For cities are wrought
  Of the stuff of the world's live brain.
Cities are thin veils, woven of thought,
  And thought, breaking, rends them in twain.)

And the fens were not. (For fens are dreams
  Dreamt by a race long dead;
And the earth is naught, and the sun but seems:
  And so those who know have said.)

So veil beyond veil illimitably lifted:
  And I saw the world's naked face,
Before, reeling and baffled and blind, I drifted
  Back within the bounds of space.

*

I have forgot the unforgettable.
  All of honey and milk the air is.
God send I do forget . . . The merry winds swell
  In the scarlet gowns bound for St Mary's.

Along with the eeriness and bewilderment, however, Rose's first collection of poems contains another dominant note. There is an especial emphasis on compassion, and the word 'pity' recurs throughout the book.

Let us come, you and I, where the roads run blind,
  Out beyond the transient city,
That our love, mingling with earth, may find
  Her imperishable heart of pity.

Shortly after *The Two Blind Countries* was out Rose decided to throw a small party at her flat, and greatly daring she wrote to invite Walter de la Mare. 'I wonder if Miss Royde-Smith said anything to you about my flat-warming', she asked. 'Anyhow . . .

I would be most proud if you would come, could you?... I don't know where you are, but this would be forwarded from almost anywhere, I suppose – such is fame.' To Rose's joy he did come, as also did Naomi, and Rupert too, just back from the South Seas, as well as Frank Sidgwick (Rose's new publisher) and various other friends. 'It wasn't an ambitious party', she recalled in 'Coming to London'. 'There wasn't much to eat or drink, so far as I remember, but we played paper games and it was great fun at the time, and part of the sociable London life which seemed so happy, clever, exciting and good.' That party took place exactly five weeks before the outbreak of war.

So far as we know Rose hardly saw Rupert again once war began. By now he was a literary lion, and besides was much occupied with Cathleen Nesbitt. But we may guess, from Rose's eighth novel, *Non-Combatants and Others*, which she wrote just after Rupert's death in 1915, that she did encounter him at least a couple more times. *Non-Combatants* was the first of Rose's books in which the central figure was a woman, and she showed 'Alix' as secretly in love with 'Basil Doye', a brilliant young artist. Basil, who had enjoyed a flirtation with Alix before the war, but had then dropped her, resembles Rupert in many ways. In wartime London, when they meet by chance, Basil finds himself almost bored with her. 'Alix wasn't really altogether what he wanted. She was too nervy ... However, they had always amused each other; she was clever, and nice to look at; he remembered vaguely that he had been a little in love with her once, before the war. If the war hadn't come just then, he might have become a great deal in love with her. Before the war one had wanted a rather different sort of person, of course, from now; more of a companion, to discuss things with.' A little later there is another meeting, a tête-à-tête in a flat near Chancery Lane. Alix, who a few days earlier had caught sight of Basil embracing a radiant young beauty, is tortured by jealousy, and even though Basil himself admits that her rival 'doesn't care a hang', she impulsively declares her own love. 'She doesn't care a hang', Alix echoed, 'But I do. Oh, Basil, I do.' The scene is drawn with extreme poignancy. After a moment of silence 'Basil looked swiftly at Alix, and Alix saw horror in his eyes before he veiled it. The next moment it was veiled: veiled by his quick, friendly smile. He leant forward and took her outstretched hands in his, and spoke lightly, easily. He did it well; few people could have attained at once to such ease, such spontaneous naturalness of affection. "Why, of course – I know. The way you and I care for each other is one of the best things I've got in my life. It lasts too, when the other sorts of caring go phut".' They talked of other things, and he told her that his battalion might be sent abroad, perhaps to south-east Europe. Alix managed to keep control of herself until he left, but then, after she had heard his steps running down the wooden stairs she let go 'and was submerged by the cold, engulfing seas'. The symbolism of cold engulfing seas occurs again when Alix is told that her younger brother has been killed in France. 'The horror rose and loomed over her, like a great wave towering, just going to break. "But – but – but" she stammered, and put out her hands, keeping it off – "But he hadn't lived yet . . ." Then the wave broke, like a storm crashing on a ship at sea.'

That was written in 1916, when Rupert's death was still, for many, an open wound. But for Rose it was a wound which over the years healed without a scar. Just after the end of the second world war, in a letter to one of her friends, Roger Senhouse, she wrote of Rupert with affection but with entire detachment: 'I often wonder what would Rupert have turned into if he'd lived? An outmoded elderly poet? Or would he have left poetry and been a scholar-don? He was a charming creature.'

6

DAUGHTER AT HOME

AT SHELFORD, where the Macaulays lived a more or less conventional life, as befitted the family of a Cambridge don, Rose continued to play the part of a daughter at home during the years just before the war came. It was now accepted that she should give a good deal of time to her writing, but in spite of this she was in effect a slave to her mother, who since Aulay's death had become neurotically demanding. Friends and relations regarded the family as happily united and in a sense they were, nevertheless the atmosphere at Southernwood was seldom lacking in tension. If Grace Macaulay did not get her way at once everyone suffered for it. Jean, who was occasionally home for a few days' leave,[1] can remember that their father, as he grew older, was often even more silent than usual. Although devoted to their mother he tried to avoid discussions with her, or if they were inevitable he refrained from arguing, simply because he preferred peace and quiet.

Rose, when things were too difficult, disappeared for long country walks. But it must not be imagined that the years at Southernwood brought her nothing but frustration. Especially positive and rewarding were the developments in her whole attitude towards religion that came about during this time. On Sundays at Shelford churchgoing was of course taken entirely for

[1] She had completed her hospital training in 1909 and then taken up district nursing, in company with a fellow nurse, Annie ('Nancy') Willetts, who became her lifelong friend and companion.

granted and Rose was always in the family pew. But when the Macaulays were first at Southernwood this churchgoing, as well as family prayers, had been for her chiefly a matter of habit and good manners. After Aulay's murder however, while she was still prostrate with grief, she was much comforted and helped (as also were her mother and Margaret) by a gifted local clergyman, F. H. A. Williams, the High Church vicar of nearby Sawston. Doubtless with his encouragement, as she approached the age of thirty, Rose found herself becoming an ardent Anglo-Catholic (though always an unorthodox one), making regular use of the confessional – she came to regard Absolution as an indispensable part of the sacramental life – and also attending retreats. According to Jean, and Dorothea Conybeare has confirmed this, Mr Williams was the first really formative religious influence in Rose's life. But her leanings were already in the High Church direction, at least as regards externals. The adjuncts of Catholic worship, the chanting and the incense, the candles glowing in mysterious dimness, the dignified ritual of the Mass – all of these attracted her strongly, reminding her as they did of Varazze. Yet it should be emphasised that she was not drawn towards Rome itself. She regarded many Roman doctrines as irrational, and her ideas of Catholicism were inevitably coloured by what she had seen of it as a child, when the Macaulay sisters were treated as heretics at the convent school. Doubtless, too, she had been influenced by her mother's attitude of scorn towards the superstition and naive legalism of the Italian peasants.

Another facet of Rose's reaction to Aulay's death was a longing to dedicate herself to some form of service, and she offered herself as a potential missionary to the Universities' Mission to Central Africa. She was not accepted, on grounds that she was not 'balanced' enough, but nearer at hand there were lesser opportunities, and she took to district visiting and teaching in the local Sunday school. She also participated in a scheme for settling waifs and strays with village families whereby she 'adopted' an orphan called Arthur. The little boy lived in Shelford with foster parents, and Rose paid for his keep and sometimes took him out. It is said that Arthur was very happy, and that Rose tried to teach him to tell the truth, but unfortunately we do not know what became of him, or what were his memories of his benefactress.

In the meantime, as far as the intellectual aspects of religion were concerned, Rose was reaching out in new directions. She became addicted to sermons and before long made a habit of going into Cambridge, sometimes with her mother and Margaret, to hear various High Church preachers, especially Father Waggett, the Cowley Father. This remarkable mission priest became a family friend, and was much beloved by Rose herself. 'He used to call me "the hockey girl"', she remembered long afterwards, 'because of sometimes meeting me coming in with my hockey stick after some match . . . He was the most brilliant and enchanting person. We used sometimes to sit under him at St Giles's; he could, by the turn of a phrase, set the whole congregation laughing (which he once said he deplored, but I think can't have).'[1] Father Waggett was a stimulating and cheering influence and he was also, for Rose, the starting point of an enduring connection with the Cowley Fathers. It was after becoming friends with him that she started making her confessions at their centre in London (St Edward's House, Westminster). Father Lucius Cary was her first confessor there.

Such then was the tenor of Rose's newly found religious practice during the last pre-war years; its pattern fitted well with her life at Shelford and with the irksome role of daughter at home. From 1912 onwards she was indeed the *only* Macaulay daughter at home: hitherto she had been able to count upon Margaret to share the filial burden.[2] But since Aulay's death

[1] *Letters to a Friend*, p. 40.
[2] Even Eleanor was now out of reach; when she finished training as a teacher in 1912 she went to India. For five years she taught in Lahore, and then became a missionary with the Society for the Propagation of the Gospel.

Margaret, who was by temperament impatient, had been finding her mother's company an almost unbearable strain. For a time she tried to distract herself by working on a schoolbook for children[1] and then on a novel.[2] But writing was obviously not her métier, and instead she turned more and more to parish work. Accompanied by a Shelford friend, Maisie Candy, she took to assisting, from time to time, at a mission house in Bethnal Green belonging to the East London Deaconesses, for like Rose she had felt impelled towards some form of self-dedication. Finally she decided to offer herself as a probationer deaconess (she was ordained in 1913). It was a brave plunge, partly because she had doubts as to whether she could adapt to community life, but also because she knew how her mother would react. Unable to face the inevitable explosion, she wrote from London to break the news, and it was poor Rose who had to cope with the tears and hysterics. Later on, when Grace Macaulay had become used to the idea of Margaret being a deaconess she was quite proud of her and took much interest in her work (there had been the same sequence of reactions when Jean left home). But at the time she thought she was heartbroken.

Margaret's departure for Bethnal Green did not mean that she was never at Shelford, for her mother made such a fuss that she was given special permission to make frequent visits home. Nevertheless Rose, from this time onwards, was her mother's most immediate target. This was a gratuitous misfortune. She craved independence just as much as her sisters did, but she lacked their worthy pretexts for withdrawing out of range. Novels – so it could be argued, by Rose's uncles, for example – could just as well be written at Shelford as anywhere else.

Rose's plight seems to have touched the heart of her father, for several times during the years just before the war he took her

---

[1] *Stories from Chaucer* (Cambridge University Press, 1911).
[2] *The Sentence Absolute* (James Nisbet, 1914).

away with him for holidays that gave her a complete change of scene. These were happy interludes for both of them. They understood one another well, and in some ways were temperamentally alike. A Hellenic cruise in the spring of 1912 was one of the most memorable of these holiday trips. Never before had Rose travelled east of Italy, and the joy of her first taste of Greece and the Greek islands shines out in a short story called 'The Empty Berth' which she wrote soon afterwards (it was published the following year in the *Cornhill Magazine*, and described by Edward Conybeare as 'a weird and original ghost story'). Rose and her father were in congenial company, which included the Headmaster of Eton, Dr Edward Lyttelton, and five Eton housemasters, all with their families, as well as Logan Pearsall Smith and Jane Harrison the Newnham anthropologist.

Two of their fellow passengers with whom Rose and her father made special friends were an Irish judge, Sir John Ross, and his son Ronald, who was then twenty-three and reading for the Bar. There was a sequel to this holiday friendship. Four months later Rose was invited to join a small house-party at Dunmoyle, the Ross estate in Northern Ireland. It was an invitation which of course aroused Grace Macaulay's matchmaking hopes. Engagements and marriages were in the air: Margaret's friend Maisie Candy had married a curate the previous year, and more recently Rose had been bridesmaid to Gladys Fanshawe when she married another parson, a Macaulay cousin. There was a flurry of preparations for the Irish visit, and Jean was told by her mother in confidence that an engagement was almost certainly imminent. But we have no reason to suspect that Rose herself (nor indeed Ronnie Ross) had any such thoughts. Besides this it seems that ever since Somerville Rose had been convinced that marriage was a second-best to a career. Certainly at this time she held a jaundiced view of it; in no less than four of her early novels she portrayed unhappy marriages.

In addition to the Hellenic cruise, another holiday that Rose shared with her father just before the war, in fact during the summer of 1914, was a trip to western Canada to visit Will, who by now, at thirty, had a farm of his own in the wilds of Alberta. The Macaulays, like so many others, appear to have had no inkling that war was near, at least so far as Britain was concerned, for Rose and her father set off across the Atlantic in mid-July, only three weeks before war was declared.

We know nothing of Rose's impressions of Canada, but the story of a hairbreadth escape that she had during her time at Gibbons, Alberta, became a family legend. While Will was busy harvesting she and her father went off for a walk and decided to follow the railway track. In a narrow cutting with almost vertical sides they suddenly realised that a train was rushing towards them. Sprinting desperately for a recess they reached it only just in time. In addition to this story, only one fragment has survived from the Canadian visit, a snapshot of Rose and her father with Will outside the simple clapboard house that he had built with his own hands. The place was obviously a bachelor establishment and Will preferred it that way. He was always being told by his family that he needed a wife; Grace Macaulay thought that Jean's friend Nancy Willetts would suit him well. But although in theory he was not averse to matrimony, and he doted on children (the young families of his Gibbons neighbours adored him) he was secretly, so Jean believes, afraid of marriage – as indeed were many of the Macaulays – and excused himself, with his usual banter, by insisting that life in the Canadian outback was far too rough and hard for any English girl.

Six weeks after the outbreak of war Rose and her father arrived back in England on board a British liner, the *Laconia*, disguised as a Dutch vessel. Will followed, to join up, as soon as the harvest was over. To Rose the war came as a horrifying bombshell – her attitude towards the outside world during the pre-war years had been one of soaring hope and optimism. But much more personal distresses were to strike her down within a matter of months. First, in April 1915, there was Rupert's death and then in July her father, by this time nearly sixty-three, and on the point of resigning his lectureship to concentrate on the more leisurely research he loved, suffered a serious stroke and died a few days later.

At the funeral at Shelford only Margaret and Jean were able to represent the immediate family (Jean had dashed back from France where she and Nancy Willetts were now with the French Red Cross). Will, by this time an officer in the King's Royal Rifles, was at the front. Eleanor was in India. Their mother was completely incapacitated by grief and Rose herself was likewise unable to face appearing in public.

When Rose lost her father she lost the anchor of her life. She had indeed loved him as a person, but over and above her daughterly affection she had looked to his ethical standards as her ultimate moral yardstick. And his characteristic qualities of simplicity, gentleness and reserve, his love of truth and his logical mind, had all of them combined to form her ideal.

Shortly before her father's death Rose had embarked on her first experiment in war work. In the hopes that it would keep her thoughts off the war she had volunteered as a V.A.D. nurse. But according to Jean this was a mad choice, for Rose (alone among the Macaulays) was hyper-sensitive to physical pain and also uncontrollably squeamish; she tended to vomit or faint at the sight of blood or the mere mention of horrors.

In May 1915 a big modern house called Mount Blow, on the Gogmagog Hills outside Cambridge, was adapted as a military convalescent home; it was one of the many emergency war hospitals around Cambridge. Soon afterwards Rose began her part-time work there, and Edward Conybeare noted in his diary that she was now 'a scrubber'. So it was during the stricken months after her father's death that she was plunged into the novitiate of hospital work. As might have been expected it was intensely uncongenial to her, and in the novel she was currently writing, *Non-Combatants and Others*, she vented her distaste and resentment. There she described the long hours of standing, the unbearable sights and sounds, the hospital smells and the 'unreasonable' hospital rules.

Rose was not a success as a nurse; even as a scrubber she did the wrong thing. Her long skirts were quickly soaked because she had not thought of working backwards as she scrubbed, and this earned her a sharp reproof; she was ordered to *re*cede not to *pro*ceed in future. There is also a story that in a ward where each man's boots were kept at the bottom of the bed she scrubbed carefully round each pair. She did stupid things, too, in the kitchen, and was reprimanded because a saltcellar on a patient's tray was untidy. But despite all this she persevered for about six months. In a wintertime photograph of staff and patients on the Mount Blow terrace she is just recognisable as she sits hunched and miserable in her thin uniform, a starched cap pulled down on her head.

By February 1916 she had abandoned nursing and thrown herself into a very different kind of work. This time she was a land-girl, to the astonishment of Uncle Edward, who commented with pained surprise 'Rose M . . . is now *spreading manure*!!' That winter was an especially icy one, but even in a blizzard the rough outdoor labour was more to Rose's taste than the pettiness and drudgery of the hospital. As yet there was no Women's Land Army, but already quite a few women were replacing men who had been called up. One of the Macaulays' Shelford friends, Margaret Stewart-Roberts, daughter of a former Master of Caius, had been working on the land for some months when Rose followed her example.

At Station Farm, close to Great Shelford, Rose was taken on by the farmer, Peter Grain, on a friendly basis. She was already a familiar figure on his land, for before the war she had often gone striding past it, up on to the Gogs, with her dog Tom.[1] Peter Grain's wife, who herself sometimes joined in the land work, recalls that in those days there was no mechanisation whatever at Station Farm. The most backbreaking labour of all was the hoeing. Rose wrote of it at the time in some verses entitled 'Hoeing the Wheat'. These she put, along with some others about her experiences at Station Farm, under the heading 'On the Land, 1916',[2] and together they give a vivid impression of what it was like to be one of the early land-girls. 'Driving Sheep' tells of a cold Cambridgeshire daybreak, when the 'sheep-women' arrive, frozen and only half awake, to let out the flock, afterwards driving the sheep, with 'their lilting bleat, their sharp scuttling feet' towards a new feeding-ground near Grantchester. Then in 'Spreading Manure' Rose compared the plight of herself and her companions to that of the soldiers in the Flanders mud, and two further poems are autumnal, recalling bonfires on the stubble and the camaraderie of a midday picnic after a morning of pulling potatoes, when Rose and the others, in a shadowed ditch, make 'a peaceful circle of food, drink, smoke and mirth'. Rose obviously enjoyed working on the land. A snapshot taken by Dorothea Conybeare in the spring of 1916 shows her looking happy and free and easy, as surrounded by four other land-girls she takes a swig from a bottle, while her friends look on, much amused at her 'unladylike' behaviour.

Rose's mother always relished moving house, and within a few months of becoming a widow she decided that she must leave the

---

[1] She was very fond of Tom, a mongrel who was partly Chow. Tom had a snappish temper and at Southernwood often flew at visitors' dogs and sometimes the visitors themselves. Edward Conybeare records having been bitten by 'Rose's beastly Chow', and also that on another occasion R.M. herself was bitten 'in fighting Tom's battles'.

[2] They were published in her second book of poetry *Three Days* (1919).

Cambridge area. Apparently she felt that the family's new home should be nearer to London – 'for Rose's sake'.[1] Perhaps Rose already envisaged applying for a war job in one of the Ministries, since by 1916 a register of university women had been compiled, and a project for employing women graduates in the Civil Service had been officially sanctioned. The Macaulays looked first of all at houses in Chigwell and Broxbourne, possibly with the idea that Margaret's visits from Bethnal Green would be easier if they remained the same side of London. And Rose, who at the time had a sentimental affection for Liverpool Street Station (in *Non-Combatants* she wrote that 'as the jumping-off place for East Anglia . . . [it] has a soothing power of its own') may not have been averse to suburban Essex. But when eventually, in August 1916, a house to everyone's liking was found, it was not on the eastern side of London but at Beaconsfield. This meant, for Rose, the prospect of glorious walks through Burnham Beeches, as well as of easy access to London. She counted on long country walks as much as ever, yet London still drew her irresistibly; there, in spite of all the wartime uprootings, many of the friends with whom she was happiest, including Naomi Royde-Smith, still met and gossiped and exchanged ideas very much as usual.

London was also important to her because of her link with the Cowley Fathers in Westminster. Since the beginning of the war Father Cary had been mostly in Oxford, so Rose had been seeing another confessor, Father Johnson, one of his younger colleagues. Father Johnson, a cousin of John Cowper Powys, was a priest with rare pastoral gifts, and more than thirty years later he was to play a part of such supreme importance in Rose's life, by means of a very unusual transatlantic correspondence, that the few details which are known of their early connection must be recorded here.

Rose did not see Father Johnson very often, probably not more

[1] R.M. had by this time given up her flat.
[2] The Rev. John Hamilton Cowper Johnson, 1877–1961.

than about half a dozen times during the first two years of the war (the time during which she suffered the loss of her father). And then, in the autumn of 1916, he was transferred to the American branch of his Order so their relationship came to an end. But his ministry as confessor, though brief, made an indelible impression on Rose, as she herself told him long afterwards: 'You know, I remember you very well thirty-six years ago . . . You had gentleness, and understanding, and sympathy, and were infinitely helpful and intelligent in advice. And said quite a lot; which I liked . . . [and] it was obvious that you had a sense of humour . . . I can say now that I was very sorry when you disappeared, and when dear Father Cary returned to take his own people over, good as he was. You had supplied something rather different.'[1]

Apart from the confessional there was only one occasion when Rose and Father Johnson met. Only once, during the whole course of their lives, did they converse face to face. Before he left England she attended a retreat which he conducted at a convent somewhere in the London suburbs. After her death Father Johnson described his memories of it, or rather of what he saw of Rose while the retreat was in progress, and his account provides a brief but telling glimpse of Rose as she was at the age of thirty-five. When she came into the conductor's room for her interview, the two sat upright on chairs facing one another, 'both of us stiff and shy – much more stiff and shy than in the addresses in the little chapel, talking, I think, of nothing save only of how a young lady living with her family might most suitably conduct herself . . . Oh yes, and I remember looking out from the little parlour where I was put, into the little, dull square garden, and seeing Miss Macaulay pacing up and down very gravely and slowly, I think *on the grass*, for a long while, in *steadily drizzling rain*, tall and grave and thoughtful, wearing some sort of dark tweed

[1] *Letters to a Friend*, p. 227.

suit – no overcoat or rain-coat. This she did for a long time.'[1]

The move to Beaconsfield took place just before the end of 1916, and early in the new year Rose began work as a temporary civil servant. Her first post was as a junior administrative assistant in the War Office, in a department dealing with exemptions from military service; she herself was concerned with conscientious objectors. No records of her work have survived, but one of her contemporaries, Dame Myra Curtis, who was at the time in another Government department later said she remembered hearing it said that Rose was 'rather hampered' by an inability to keep an individual note out of her minutes. 'Which seems quite probable', she added, 'and much to her credit, since a gifted writer ought not to be good at stodgy Civil Service minutes.'

Throughout 1917 Rose's routine was extremely strenuous: according to Edward Conybeare it meant working ten hours a day, while her commuting took three hours more. During the week she can have had little time for anything else, but at week-ends she was able to let up a little, and occasionally stayed with Naomi Royde-Smith at her cottage at Holmbury in north Sussex. After one of these visits, writing to Walter de la Mare, she described the woodland near Naomi's cottage as 'the peace-fullest and silentest and sweetest-smelling place anywhere'. But she did not always find the Holmbury woods so soothing. They were the background for one of the most heartrending of the few poems she wrote about the war, 'Picnic, July 1917'.

> We lay and ate sweet hurt-berries
> In the bracken of Hurt Wood.
> Like a quire of singers singing low
> The dark pines stood.

[1] See letter from Father Johnson to C.B.S., 6 August 1959 (*Letters to a Friend*, pp. 17–18).

Behind us climbed the Surrey Hills,
    Wild, wild in greenery;
At our feet the downs of Sussex broke
    To an unseen sea.

And life was bound in a still ring,
    Drowsy, and quiet, and sweet . . .
When heavily up the south-east wind
    The great guns beat.

We did not wince, we did not weep,
    We did not curse or pray;
We drowsily heard, and someone said,
    'They sound clear to-day'.

We did not shake with pity and pain,
    Or sicken and blanch white.
We said, 'If the wind's from over there
    There'll be rain to-night'.

*

Once pity we knew, and rage we knew,
    And pain we knew, too well,
And we stared and peered dizzily
    Through the gates of hell.

But now hell's gates are an old tale;
    Remote the anguish seems;
The guns are muffled and far away,
    Dreams within dreams.

And far and far are Flanders mud,
    And the pain of Picardy;
And the blood that runs there runs beyond
    The wide waste sea.

We are shut about by guarding walls;
  (We have built them lest we run
Mad from dreaming of naked fear
  And of black things done.)

We are ringed all round by guarding walls,
  So high, they shut the view.
Not all the guns that shatter the world
  Can quite break through.

*

Oh, guns of France, oh, guns of France,
  Be still, you crash in vain . . .
Heavily up the south wind throb
  Dull dreams of pain . . .

Be still, be still, south wind, lest your
  Blowing should bring the rain . . .
We'll lie very quiet on Hurt Hill,
  And sleep once again.

Oh, we'll lie quite still, nor listen nor look,
  While the earth's bounds reel and shake,
Lest, battered too long, our walls and we
  Should break . . . should break . . .

PART II

Cross-Currents
1918 – 1942

7

FALLING IN LOVE

ROSE FIRST MET the man who was later to be the most important person in her life when she was thirty-six, and when early in 1918 she was transferred from the War Office to the new Ministry of Information. With her fluent Italian she was well qualified to work in the Italian Section of the Department for Propaganda in Enemy Countries, which had just been set up at Crewe House under Lord Northcliffe (Italy was then helping to launch Allied propaganda through Austria). The Department attracted many writers – H. G. Wells headed the German Section for a short time, and Wickham Steed was Lord Northcliffe's political adviser – and the head of the Italian Section, Gerald O'Donovan, was like Rose a novelist, though in his case the writing of novels was quite a recent development; earlier he had done various different kinds of work, and as a young man in Ireland he had been a Catholic priest. Before long Rose and he were being seen about together, for example at the lunches that were given each week by Reeve Brooke (a cousin of Rupert's who was a Civil Service 'regular') at his rooms in the Temple. Others who came to these lunches were Dorothy Lamb (a sister of Henry Lamb the artist) who had worked with Rose at the War Office, Naomi Royde-Smith and Walter de la Mare, Charles Evans of Heinemanns, Dominick Spring-Rice (then with the *Morning Post*) and Mary Agnes Hamilton, later a Labour M.P.[1]

Dark, shortish and broadshouldered, Gerald was forty-five when Rose met him, a man who aroused strong likes and dislikes.

[1] M. A. Hamilton, *Remembering my Good Friends* (1944).

Some of those who remember him in his days at Crewe House, and later, have testified to his kind impulses as well as to his ability as an organiser, and even those who did not take to him have admitted that he had exceptional charm, with his melodious voice, eloquent blue eyes, and quick incisive wit.

'Jerry,' as some of his friends called him, originally came from a humble home in County Cork, where before his birth his mother had dedicated him to the priesthood. He had been given the baptismal name of Jeremiah, and from the age of twenty-five for six years (1897–1903) the Rev. Jeremiah O'Donovan was curate and then parish priest at Loughrea, a small town in Galway. Then, apparently, he was moved elsewhere for a short time – in the *Irish Catholic Directory* for 1905 he was still listed as a priest – and soon afterwards he left the priesthood, for reasons that have not been certainly established. But to judge from his novels, which are anticlerical in tone and full of disillusionment, rebellion against the Church was one of the main reasons if not the only one. His successful first novel *Father Ralph*,[1] a book with an autobiographical flavour, showed a sincere young priest renouncing his orders as a final gesture of revolt against the corruption and obscurantism he had met within the Church.

Gerald made good in secular life to a certain extent, thanks to his intelligence and charm, but he moved from job to job, first in Dublin, then briefly in America, finally in London. A friend of his who knew him well (the late Marjorie Grant Cook, a Canadian-born novelist) believed that he suffered from deep unspoken regrets on account of having left the priesthood. One of the posts he held in London before the First World War was as a sub-warden at Toynbee Hall. He was there for just over a year, from the spring of 1910, and his appointment overlapped with Clement Attlee's secretaryship. In the official history of the Settlement[2] he is described as 'a brilliant young Irishman with a

[1] Published by Macmillan in 1913.
[2] J. A. R. Pimlott, *Toynbee Hall* (1935).

critical mind and a wide knowledge of the world'. It was half-way
through his time at Toynbee Hall, in October 1910, that Gerald
was married, at the Whitechapel registry office, to the daughter
of an Irish Protestant colonel. She was thirteen years younger
than him and had been brought up in Italy. During the next few
years a son and two daughters were born.

Towards the end of the war Rose wrote a novel called *What Not*[1]
which reflected her experiences in Government offices (it was
published by Constable, who in 1919 also brought out another
book of hers, a collection of poems entitled *Three Days*). *What
Not* was a lively though rather far-fetched skit on bureaucracy.
But the mockery missed fire because it was combined with an
earnest love story.[2] By the time *What Not* was completed Rose
was herself in love.

The love story in *What Not* concerns 'Kitty', a young lady
working in a fictitious ministry, of which 'Chester', the hero, is
Minister. Both are unattached and they long to marry but
cannot, because of various arbitrary laws and taboos, appropriate
to the fictitious situation. Rose's accounts of the early stages of
their love, and especially of the heroine's feelings, are touchingly
revealing. 'It's queer, isn't it, how strong it is', Kitty exclaims,
'this odd, desperate wanting of one person out of all the world.
It's an extraordinary, enormously strong thing.' Mutual attraction
had first stirred in them when they were week-end guests at a
friend's house in the country.

They did not talk shop, but they were linked by the strong
bond of shop shared and untalked. There was between them
the relationship ... of a government official to his intelligent

---

[1] The source of the book's title was a statement by a defendant in a food-
hoarding case: 'It has become a fine thing if people cannot live in their homes
without ... your Food Orders and What Not.'
[2] R.M. made light of this to her publisher: 'People ought to take it not
as a story but as a satire – the intelligent ones do, of course.'

subordinates . . . But this evening, as they talked, it became apparent to Kitty that, behind the screen of this relationship, so departmental, so friendly, so emptied of sex, a relationship quite other and more personal and human, which had come into embryo being some weeks ago, was developing with rapidity . . . Next morning Chester asked her to come [for] a walk with him, and on the walk the new relationship burgeoned like flowers in spring . . . when Kitty was talking he watched her with a curious, interested, pleased look . . . After tea . . . they sat in a beech wood together . . . And after dinner, when they said good-night . . . the look in his eyes . . . sent Kitty up to bed with the staggering perception of the dawning of a new and third relationship.

The ring of first-hand experience sounds again and again as Rose follows the new relationship step by step. Kitty, shrinking from the impulse to ignore accepted standards, suggests that they should try to be 'just friends'. Needless to say this does not work. 'I can't go on any longer with this – this farce', Chester burst out. 'We must end it . . . we've got to be more to each other – or less . . . We've reached the breaking point; I can't bear any more . . . We'd better not meet. What's the good of meeting, just to repeat this sort of scene again and again, and hurt each other?' They then try not meeting, but when this also fails – for they are still in the same office – Kitty broods despairingly on their situation.

When two people who love each other work in the same building . . . they disturb each other, are conscious of each other's nearness . . . There was no getting away . . . no peace of mind, none of the old careless, light-hearted living and working; nothing but a continual disturbing, restless, aching want . . . What was it, this extraordinary driving pressure of emotion, this quite disproportionate desire for companionship with, for contact with, one person out of all the world of people and things, which made, while it lasted, all other

desires, all other emotions, pale and faint beside it?...
Desire for a person ... When it came into play, principle,
chivalry, common sense, intellect, humour, culture, sweet-
ness and light, all we call civilisation, might crumple up like
match-board so this one overwhelming desire, shared by all
the animal creation, might be satisfied. On this rock the
world, the pathetic, eager, clever, foolish, so heavily handi-
capped world, might be wrecked. It was, perhaps, this one
thing that would always prevent humanity from being, in
fact, a clever and successful race, would always keep them
down somewhere near the level of the other animals.

For some months after the Armistice Rose worked on in
London. The Propaganda Department at Crewe House was
wound up at the end of 1918, and the final part of her time as a
temporary civil servant was probably spent at the Ministry of
Information's main office in Norfolk Street off the Strand. At
this point she also busied herself as a publisher's reader: when the
war ended she accepted an invitation from Constable to help in
vetting their fiction manuscripts.

Then in the spring of 1919, when the influenza epidemic
reached its climax, she succumbed and afterwards had some sort
of nervous breakdown. The accumulated stresses in her life were
more than she could bear: the long-drawn-out agony of the war,
the hard labour of her various jobs, the uncertainties of her
writing (*What Not* had a mediocre press), the grind of commuting
between Beaconsfield and London, the strain of living with her
mother, her distress on account of Will, who was severely
wounded only a few weeks before the war ended, and besides all
this, of course, the anguish of conscience caused by the fact that
she was in love with a married man.

Through the summer months she recuperated, but it was a
trying period. 'It ought to have been a time for great enterprises
and beginnings', she later wrote of this first post-war summer,

'but it emphatically wasn't. It was a queer, inconclusive, lazy, muddled, reckless, unsatisfactory, rather ludicrous time . . . We were like bankrupts, who cannot summon energy to begin life and work again in earnest.'[1] Nevertheless she did summon enough energy to write a few bitter, almost despairing poems, the last, so far as we know, that she wrote for many years. One of them, commemorating the signing of the Versailles Treaty, 'Peace. June 28th 1919', showed that the massacres of the Western Front were still a haunting nightmare to her:

> . . . There's no peace so quiet, so lasting
> As the peace you keep in France.

To what extent did this time of abject depression affect Rose's looks? She was now nearing forty, and it does seem that she was dreading the onset of middle age. In *Dangerous Ages*, which was written soon after this, a woman in her forties breaks down from overwork, and then experiences the shock of realising that her looks are suddenly fading.

She stopped before the looking-glass. Her face looked back at her, white and thin, almost haggard, traced in the last few weeks for the first time with definite lines round brow and mouth. 'Middle age' . . . a cold hand was laid round her heart. 'It had to come some time, and this illness has opened the door to it. Or shall I look young again when I'm quite well. No, never young again.' She shivered.

Doubtless Rose looked haggard and miserable while she was actually ill, but there is plenty of evidence that when once more in normal health any incipient wrinkles were discounted by her energy and zest. The memories of her at this time that have remained with her friends are of a woman almost boyish in her youthfulness. It suited her to have her hair cut short in the new fashion, and a contemporary account in the *Westminster Gazette* speaks of her 'delightful little head covered with the softest curls'.

[1] *Potterism*, p. 53.

Her wiry figure and coltish movements also had a certain charm: 'She is tall, very slight in build, with a tendency to tie herself into knots, and yet graceful with the strong grace of the born walker.' But her most striking qualities were her 'gift of laughter', 'the extraordinary nimbleness of her mind', and above all the rapidity of her staccato speech and her movements. 'Her energy is amazing . . . her face, at once worn and yet retaining the inexpressible candour of a child about the large, wide-open, heavily-lidded eyes, blue as the eyes of the adult are rarely blue, suggests this ageless energy . . . every action is with her quicker than it is with most of us . . . [and] not until you have listened to Miss Macaulay's conversation can you fully appreciate what . . . "talking nineteen to the dozen" . . . means.'

Rose was by nature resilient, both physically and mentally, and this is witnessed by the speed with which she recovered from her nervous breakdown. During the latter part of the summer of 1919 she went with Margaret and Will, who was out of hospital between operations,[1] to stay with Regi Macaulay in Argyllshire, and it must have been very soon after her return from Scotland that she was once more living her usual life, with a new novel well under way. It was to be a satire on the popular press, and Rose called it *Potterism*; she derived this word from the name of a fictitious newspaper magnate, 'Mr Potter', and it signified all the attitudes engendered by the 'Potter press', such as commercialism, vulgarity and inaccuracy.

Potterism was the first of Rose's 'middle-period' novels, those topical comedies which during the 1920s and '30s caused the name of Rose Macaulay to be more and more widely identified with a unique blend of astringent derision, gaiety, and clear-sighted observation of the current scene. And it was a landmark in Rose's

---

[1] He had lost his left lung from poisoning after a gunshot wound and his left arm was more or less paralysed. In the spring of 1920 however he returned to Canada and resumed his farming, in spite of his disability.

life comparable to the landmark in the life of an actress when her name first appears in lights. For it was her first best-seller, both in Britain and in America. *Potterism* sold well partly because it came out at just the right moment. In 1919 salty humour was precisely to the taste of the more selective reading public: laughter, especially mocking laughter with a touch of cynicism, was a pleasant escape from the intolerable post-war mess.

The inspiration for *Potterism*, as well as for the majority of Rose's ensuing novels – *Dangerous Ages, Mystery at Geneva, Told by an Idiot, Orphan Island, Crewe Train, Keeping up Appearances, Staying with Relations, Going Abroad, I would be Private* – can be attributed very largely to the influence of Gerald. We know that from *Potterism* onwards, so far as her light fiction was concerned, Rose habitually relied upon the stimulus of his lively mind, and the sparkle of her middle-period writings may be regarded as a reflection of his 'sardonic wit'[1] as well as of her own brilliance and sense of fun. Gerald once remarked (to Marjorie Grant Cook) that Rose had a brain like a man's, and that this was one of the things about her which particularly attracted him. But along with her objectiveness and devotion to truth there was her sensitive feminine side, and she needed masculine guidance. Such guidance was especially congenial when it came from someone like Gerald who laughed at the same jokes as she did.

She also responded to his general attitude towards the work of a writer, which was more businesslike than hers, and at about this time she decided to employ a literary agent, Curtis Brown. Gerald was probably also responsible, to some extent, for the fact that from *Potterism* onwards all Rose's fiction was published by Collins. He himself had been employed by the firm as an editor in 1917, when they opened their first London office.[2] And it seems that he must have been well impressed by what he saw of Collins, for if, when the time came, he had urged Rose to offer

[1] See p. 160 below.
[2] David Keir, *The House of Collins* (1952), p. 235.

Potterism elsewhere, she would almost certainly have done so. Her long-term faithfulness to the firm may also have been partly thanks to him, for later, after the war, he became one of their readers, with special responsibility for Rose's books.

It was chiefly in London that Rose and Gerald met, but during the early 1920s (when he was mostly in England, though often for months at a time in Italy) he occasionally put in an appearance at Beaconsfield. She did not conceal from her mother that he was married; Grace Macaulay seems to have been quite content to receive him on the footing of a professional friend of her daughter's. And evidently she also liked him as a person, for the date of his birthday, July 15th, is recorded in her book of anniversaries, and she would never have put it there if she disapproved of him. 'Mother was very illogical,' says Jean with a smile. 'If she liked people they were all white and if she disliked them they were all black.' Ever since a girl Grace Macaulay had cherished romantic ideas on platonic love, and now, in her late sixties, according to Jean, her regard for Gerald was enhanced when she came to realise that he was in love with Rose. 'Isn't it wonderful that someone should love Rose so much!' she exclaimed when she learnt that the heroine of one of Gerald's novels, *The Holy Tree*,[1] was meant to represent Rose, at least as regards her state of heart.

Jean's own attitude towards Gerald was very different from her mother's, and so too was Margaret's. Neither sister felt able to accept him, so they agreed with Rose that they would never discuss the relationship.

Rose was a dutiful daughter, indeed to those outside the family she seemed devoted. One of her friends who came quite often to Beaconsfield during the early 1920s, namely Dorothy Brooke,[2] said later that she did not recall any tensions between Rose and her

---

[1] Published by Heinemann in 1922.
[2] Formerly Dorothy Lamb. She and Reeve Brooke were married in 1920.

mother, whom she remembered as an entertaining old lady with 'flashing eyes and wonderful white hair'. Probably she saw Mrs Macaulay at her best; as so often the presence of a friend may have eased a difficult family situation. It was very different when the family was alone. As a widow Grace Macaulay became exasperating to her children. Rose especially could not abide her impulsive talk and interrupted her every few minutes. Jean, looking back to this time, observes with typical commonsense that it would have been far better for everyone if Rose had abandoned the pretence of making a home with her mother. But she clung on through some sort of pride and mistaken family loyalty, blinding herself to the fact that her mother was miserably aware of being despised. It was a painful impasse.

Dangerous Ages, published in 1921, may be regarded as an indirect but heartfelt protest against 'living at home'. In it an ageing widow, 'Mrs Hilary', a 'muddled bigot' in the eyes of her children, is held up to scorn and ridicule. When Grace Macaulay read the book in manuscript she recognised the portrait of herself and was deeply hurt. To Margaret she confided her distress, and she begged her to persuade Rose to tone 'Mrs Hilary' down. But the portrait remains a cruel one. Possibly however Rose was trying to make some sort of amends when she dedicated the book 'To my mother, Driving gaily through the adventurous middle years.'[1] She and her mother were not always at loggerheads. Something of Rose herself can be seen in one of the daughters in *Dangerous Ages* ('Nan') who, finding her mother unbearably trying, oscillates between sparring with her and making extravagant gestures of reconciliation.

Obviously it was easier to maintain friendly relations at long range. The one letter from Rose to her mother which survives from this time is spontaneously good-humoured: it includes a lively account of a conversation with her American publisher, Horace Liveright, a man well known for his flamboyance, energy,

[1] By now Grace Macaulay possessed a car, though she herself did not drive.

and initiative.[1] She had invited him to have lunch with her and Dorothy Brooke at the University Women's Club. 'Horace L', she wrote, 'spent lunch mostly persuading me to write a fine strong love-story for the American public ... Dorothy said "Anyone can write that – we look to Rose for something else, which no-one else can do", but Horace L said firmly "Rose Macaulay, Mrs Brooke, is a *great writer*. Now all great writers must deal with the greatest subject in the world, at one time or another." I said I had no ambition to be a great writer and my touch was for trivial topicalities ... but it was no use. However, he was quite agreeable, and it was an amusing lunch.'

[1] His firm, Boni and Liveright, published *Potterism* in 1920, and subsequently several more of R.M.'s novels. Their promotion of *Potterism* brought her, for the first time, into touch with American salesmanship. 'My American publishers' "big advertising campaign" ... impresses me enormously', she wrote to S. C. Roberts of the Cambridge University Press. 'They seem by these live methods to have succeeded in disposing of 20,000 copies of the book ... little did I think I should ever come to be a big success in the Middle West!'

8

THE NEW ROSE

DURING the years just after the war Rose and Naomi Royde-Smith were often together; and when Naomi moved to a largish house in Kensington, Number 44 Princes Gardens, and decided to let some of the rooms to her friends, Rose was glad to be able to take one. Thereafter until the start of 1922, when she once more acquired a London flat of her own,[1] she liked to spend a night or two each week at Naomi's, usually returning to Beaconsfield at the weekend, and sometimes taking Naomi with her.

Princes Gardens was the setting for Naomi's weekly parties, which were by now winning her the reputation of holding a salon. Though less grand than some of the parties given at this time for the celebrities of Bloomsbury, these evenings were often successful occasions, when as many as fifty or sixty guests, mostly writers and publishers but including a few civil servants, both men and women, crowded into Naomi's big drawing-room, while she and Rose, acting jointly as hostesses, received such diverse authors as Arnold Bennett, W. B. Yeats, Edith Sitwell and Aldous Huxley. One of the younger writers who sometimes came to 'Naomi's Thursdays' was Storm Jameson, and in her autobiography she has called them 'an urbane backwater of the literary establishment'. Naomi, whom she found a little formidable, she likens to a younger and more affable Queen Victoria. But by Rose, who from the first had welcomed her kindly, she was spellbound: '. . . a narrow head covered with small curls, like a Greek head in a museum, with that way she had of speaking in

[1] See p. 104 below.

arpeggios, and the lively hands, the small arched nose and pale deep-set eyes . . . One Thursday evening, I watched her with Arnold Bennett. He hung over her, mouth slightly open, like a great fish mesmerised by the flickering tongue of a water snake.' There was also, she recalls, a seemingly youthful radiance about Rose that drew all eyes; one could notice people looking round the room for her. Little wonder that Naomi, according to several accounts, became at this time intensely jealous of her former 'discovery', whose success was now eclipsing her own.

Some attributed Rose's radiance to her enjoyment of having arrived as a writer; few were aware that she was in love. Naomi, as one might expect, did know; indeed she helped when she could to make it easy for Rose and Gerald to meet. But only a handful of others came to sense the state of Rose's heart and to realise how things stood between her and Gerald. These few close friends tacitly accepted the situation, though some of them – Dorothy and Reeve Brooke, for example, and H. B. Usher of the *Westminster Gazette* and his wife Grace – did so only with regret because they did not care for Gerald and thought him unworthy of Rose. Outside her London circle, Rose spoke of her love (in 1921) to Olive Willis, who told her frankly that she ought to stop seeing Gerald; this inevitably led to a certain estrangement between her and Rose, though in spite of it they always remained friends.

Meantime, in the matter of Rose's religious practice, we know that up until 1921 or so her attachment did not reach a stage that she considered debarred her from Holy Communion. But after 1922 she felt compelled to desist from confession, and lacking Absolution she regarded herself as automatically cut off from Communion.[1] Not that this prevented her from continuing to

---

[1] By 1921 R.M. had a new confessor, Canon S. C. Carpenter. Long afterwards, in 1957, she wrote of him to Jean: 'He is nearly eighty now but very little changed . . . It was to him that I made my last confession in 1921 or 2 before giving it up for thirty years.'

take an academic interest in religion, especially in its ethical aspects, or from a certain amount of churchgoing. In one of her letters to Jean she protested that she was quite hurt because Jean had accused her of 'not attending' in church.

At some point during the first half of the 1920s – the exact date has not been established – Rose and Naomi had a violent quarrel. It came about because Naomi had been spreading untrue and damaging gossip of some kind about Rose. Subsequently, in the later 1920s, by which time Naomi had married Ernest Milton the actor, Rose did sometimes see her again. But the flare-up had irrevocably destroyed their friendship, and it left Rose tense and on her guard against gossipers. In *Crewe Train* one of the main themes is the menace of irresponsible feminine talk, the harm it does, the false relationships it leads to. And one of the central characters is a magnetic middle-aged woman, whose tongue inflicts pain and distress on all around her; she never stops imagining falsehoods, whispering that her friends are taking to drugs or drink, that their marriages are breaking up, that they are embarking on illicit liaisons.

After the breach with Naomi the centre of Rose's London life shifted from Kensington to Hampstead. By 1925 the Brookes had a house there, and Dorothy Brooke's diaries include many mentions of doings shared with Rose, such as walks over the Heath and crossword puzzle sessions: Rose seems to have been thoroughly bitten by the new craze for crosswords. One entry reads 'Dinner with Rose and Crossword puzzle party'; on this occasion the other guests were Humbert Wolfe, the Victor Gollanczs, Lancelot Sieveking, Viola Garvin and the E. V. Knoxs. Rose was also drawn to Hampstead by her friendship with Robert Lynd, literary editor of the *News Chronicle*, and his wife Sylvia; she was often at their Friday evenings in Keats Grove. 'Sylvia's Fridays' were informal parties when the guests sometimes amused themselves with guessing games and charades. Authors such as

James Joyce and Max Beerbohm occasionally turned up, and Rose could count on the company of the Gollanczs, David Lows, J. B. Priestleys, and Philip Guedallas.

It was during these same years that Rose became acquainted with some of the Bloomsbury Group, though she was never herself within it. She first met E. M. Forster at about the time when he was working on *Aspects of the Novel,* and was soon his ardent disciple. In the 1920s she knew Leonard and Virginia Woolf only slightly; it was much later that she became Virginia's affectionate friend. But a dinner party to which she invited the Woolfs in the '20s is described by Leonard in his autobiography, and his account is of note as showing the lavish scale on which Rose entertained: it was a dinner party of ten or twelve people, in a restaurant just across the road from Rose's flat. The Woolfs arrived straight from work at the Hogarth Press, unchanged and dishevelled, to find that their fellow guests were 'literary gents and ladies' including the Lynds and Conal O'Riordan, the Irish novelist, 'all immaculate in evening dress'. 'Though we loved Rose', Leonard confesses, 'it was the kind of party that both of us loathed.'

Rose's party-going at this time was not only amongst her own friends; she seems to have found pleasure and amusement even at functions to which she was invited as a public figure. One sidelight here is an entry in Dean Inge's diary which might almost be a paragraph from a gossip column: it mentions that a 'little dinner' which Mrs Inge had thought was 'one of our most successful' was attended by Rose Macaulay, an ambassador, two peeresses and a Scottish theologian.[1] There is also a revealing glimpse of Rose in one of her letters to Jean: 'I heard the King [George V] at the Royal Garden Party . . . speaking to a foreign lady of the "fundamental good sense of the English" . . . which keeps them from excitement and bloodshed; I expect he is very glad of this; kings must be. Alfonso of Spain is being tracked by

[1] *Diary of a Dean* (p. 108).

anarchists who desire his life, and no monarch but ours is very safe, I expect.'

The year 1925 was a landmark for Rose, for it was the year when her mother died, after a heart attack, and when she found herself, at forty-four, fully independent for the first time in her life. Henceforward her London flat was her only home,[1] though after the Beaconsfield ménage was wound up a new centre for the family came into being in the country. Margaret, by now no longer working in Bethnal Green, decided to move to Hampshire.[2] She lived first at Petersfield and then bought a house in the nearby village of Liss, and for the next fifteen years or so Rose and the others often spent holidays with her. Rose saw more of her, at this time, than of the others, and she later wrote 'I loved her very dearly.' According to Jean, Margaret's character had been transformed by her life in religion. Once so irritable and quick-tempered she now radiated serenity.

In London Rose found that her new independence held advantages of many kinds. For one thing she was free from living-in servants. 'What a mercy it is to be able to do with a morning char', she wrote to Jean, 'and to have such a nice one as my Mrs Trowles ... She is a very loyal charwoman, and cuts out pieces from the papers about me whenever she sees them and pastes them in a book.' It was also fun discussing the current news with Mrs Trowles and her husband, who cleaned the courtyard at St Andrew s Mansions. At the time of the General Strike Rose found that her ideas were much clearer after a few minutes' chat with Mr and Mrs Trowles than after half an hour with Sir William Beveridge. Another of the pleasures of independence was that she could listen in as much as she liked. The wireless, a new delight,

[1] She had settled at St Andrew's Mansions near Baker Street.
[2] She had retired in 1924 when the East London Diocesan Deaconess Community came to an end, though she continued to be known as 'Sister Margaret' and always wore her religious habit.

fascinated her so much that although she was not in the least musical she could sit happily through concerts if they came to her over the air.

Living alone also meant that Rose could see Gerald more often, but this did not cause her to ignore his family, in fact she was increasingly friendly to them, and her kindness and generosity were lavish. Yet during the latter part of the 1920s, to almost all of her friends – even the Brookes – as well as to her family, Rose became intensely secretive about Gerald. No doubt she missed the moral support of her mother's friendliness to him. But another reason may have been a determination not to break up his marriage. By this time she and Gerald were quite often spending holidays abroad together, and Rose took care to plan these times away as discreetly as possible. Usually Rose slipped off to meet him either before or after travelling with her sisters or with friends. Often the holidays with Gerald were in Italy or France, and several times they went to the Pyrenees. One year, after spending some time with Gerald in the south of France, chiefly at Albi, Rose went on to explore northern Bavaria and Bohemia with the Brookes. And twice she combined her private holidays with 'business visits' to Switzerland (as a special reporter for the *Daily Chronicle* she attended the second Assembly of the League of Nations in Geneva, and in 1925 she accompanied a Lunn tour to Mürren and Maloja as a guest lecturer).

If Gerald had been free, would Rose have married him? Marjorie Grant Cook thought that it would have been a disastrous mistake, for she was convinced that Rose needed independence. Jean, too, insists that it would never have suited Rose to be married. Rose herself, writing to Jean in 1926, apropos of Margaret who for a time shared her ménage with a companion, a former lay helper at Bethnal Green, remarked that she could not understand why anyone should choose to live with someone else rather than alone. There are also a few pointers in Rose's contemporary writings. One of the many light articles she wrote at this time was entitled 'People who Should Not Marry', and although mostly badinage it includes the following telling remark: 'Some men and women might well prefer to live alone, meeting their beloved only when it suits them, thus retaining both that measure of freedom (small though any human freedom is) enjoyed by the solitary, and the delicate bloom on the fruit of love which is said to be brushed off by continual contact.' Furthermore a passage in *Crewe Train* indicates that Rose held realistic views on what marriage meant for someone who was temperamentally self-sufficient. 'If you had never loved', the heroine 'Denham' reflects, almost resentfully, 'you could be happy, loafing, idle and alone, exploring new places, sufficient to yourself. Once committed to love, you couldn't; it came baldly to that . . . Love was the great taming emotion; perhaps the only taming emotion. It defeated all other desires in the end. You might struggle and rebel but in the end love got you . . . One was trapped by love, by that blind storming of the senses, by that infinite tenderness, that unreasoning, unreasoned friendship, which was love. This was the trap, this was the snare . . . Love broke one in the end, ground one down, locked the fetters on one's free limbs.'

So far as Rose's writing was concerned the 1920s were busy and stimulating years but they were also years of uneasy transition. Up until her mother's death she produced not only a novel each year – *Potterism, Dangerous Ages, Mystery at Geneva, Told by an Idiot, Orphan Island* – but also many articles and reviews, and she even found time to try her hand at a play.[1] Between 1925 and 1929 there were fewer novels, in fact only two, *Crewe Train* and *Keeping up Appearances*, but the flow of articles and reviews, in

---

[1] R.M.'s only play, *Bunkum*, was never published. Intended as a thriller, it is not an impressive piece of work. There is interest however in her choice of hero and heroine: the former is an Irish crook impersonating a parson, the latter a tomboyish *ingénue*.

response to an insistent demand, had now become a spate. Rose's journalistic style, deriding but unmalicious, and the drily mocking way in which she exposed the absurdities and inconsistencies that she saw around her, were much to the taste of the middle-brows of the period – the same middle-brows who looked forward each week to *Punch*, as indeed Rose herself did (her other favourite weekly was the *New Statesman*). But her public now included some of the lowest of low-brows, an embarrassing fact that she tried to explain away. When *Crewe Train* was serialised in *Eve* she wrote to Jean: 'I'm sorry you don't like *Eve*. I never see it. I expect it is like all those other [women's] papers. My agents sent them my novel because they wanted a new serial just then, and pay well, and they took it. Most papers reject[ed] it, as not being a good serial novel, so I was pleased. I don't expect anyone will read it there; I never knew anyone read a serial in a paper yet.'

Labelled as 'one of the most brilliant of living women writers' Rose now contributed to the *Daily Mail*, the *Daily Express* and the *Evening Standard* (though she did not confine herself to the popular press; she also wrote for periodicals such as the High Church weekly *The Guardian*). Usually she chattered away about trivialities – 'Why I dislike Cats, Clothes and Visits' – though she sometimes touched on more serious subjects, 'Class' for example, asking 'Does Ancestry Matter?' and delving into 'The Riddle of Refinement'. Occasionally too, with obvious relish, she tackled a religious theme such as 'Have we Done with Hell Fire?'.

There is no doubt that despite a certain amount of genuine enjoyment Rose was troubled by her popularity, or rather by what she felt was the prostitution of her ability as a writer. Yet she had to earn her living, or at least a large part of it, she gave generously to family and friends, she counted on holidays abroad, and the rewards of popular journalism were considerable. 'To pay – or rather, to be paid – was one of the few unimpeachable justifications for anything' – so she observed in *Keeping up*

Appearances. This novel, which was published in 1928, brought clearly to light the conflict in Rose's mind as regards her writing, for the heroine, 'Daisy Daphne,' possessed two separate personalities. Daphne, the assumed personality, was poised, resourceful, never at a loss for a quip, the friend of high-brows; Daisy, the real person, was diffident, nervy, by nature a poet, and by profession a writer of popular trash. Daisy hated herself for pandering to the imbecile tastes of her public, for being a cheap and babbling authoress: 'It was all like a foolish clattering stream, running frothing beside the real stream of life.'

But Rose was being unduly sensitive. In some quarters the best of her articles were taken seriously and much admired. In 1924 the Cambridge University Press wanted to publish a collection of them, and she would have liked to agree, but she had just accepted a similar offer from Methuen. And when the Methuen collection, *A Casual Commentary*, containing forty of her early pieces, appeared in 1925, it was presented as a book for intellectual readers, and the blurb claimed that Rose Macaulay was 'one of the most accomplished writers of essays now working. She brings to every subject wit and humour, very observant eyes, and a fearless judgment.'

Yet a more perceptive comment on Rose's writing at this time, a comment not only on her special brand of humour but also on her future potentialities, was made by Humbert Wolfe in his foreword to a collection of her poems which was included in the Benn series 'The Augustan Books of English Poetry'. Rose's wit, so he conceded, was with reason regarded as her leading characteristic. But he claimed that those who liked her work best had always been aware of something held back, some power or quality in reserve. 'They have been convinced that some day she will bring that asset into play, and they believe that it will prove to have in it as much of tears as of laughter.'

9

INTERLUDE IN AMERICA

IN SPITE OF the reorientation of Rose's personal life she was as
devoted as ever to her brother and sisters, and made a point of
writing to them regularly and seeing them as often as she could.
But with Will in Canada, Eleanor in India, and Jean tied to her
nursing, there could seldom be any family reunions. In the
summer of 1929 however an ambitious plan took shape for a
holiday that Rose was going to share with Margaret and Will (he
was still unmarried, indeed he remained a bachelor all his life).
Earlier that year Rose had been in poor health – she had shown
signs of incipient heart trouble – and she may well have felt the
need to get right away. The idea was that she and Margaret
should travel across America to meet Will on the West Coast,
and from there the three would go on together to make an
extensive motor tour of the continent. Rose had hopes that they
might reach Mexico and even Guatemala, a country which had
recently fired her imagination.

The two sisters arrived in New York in December 1929 and
set off at once on the transcontinental train journey to Portland,
Margaret, as always, wearing her Deaconess habit, a long flowing
black dress with a cord girdle. 'Everyone is very much interested
in Margaret's clothes', Rose wrote to Jean, when the journey was
nearing its end. 'The porters and waiters etc. ask what she is. The
man who sells candy on the train . . . thought we must be coming
out to do mission work . . . They are also interested in where we
come from, because of the way we talk . . . The people are very

charming . . . all most religious and scriptural; the very porter (a black) had found the Lord. In fact, I expect the only passengers who hadn't were us and a couple of Japs who played cards all day . . . Our Pullman was rather Fundamentalist on the whole; it had a loquacious minister, who once, it seemed, had "lived in sin" but now quite the contrary, ever since the Lord had spoken to him while he was getting theatre tickets at a box office and said "Touch not the unclean thing". Since then he hasn't. He and his wife were having a dispute about dancing with some other passengers, who thought it comparatively innocent. The minister condemned it utterly, and said that 90% of the criminals in U.S. gaols attributed their downfall to dancing, according to a recent questionnaire. It must obviously be prison etiquette to put that, when asked such a foolish and impertinent question.'

From Portland the three Macaulays started southwards along the Pacific coast in Will's four-seater Essex – his disabled arm did not prevent him from driving – often stopping for the night at 'camping cabins', the crude forerunners of motels. They aimed at spending Christmas either at San Diego or just over the Mexican border in Lower California. Rose hoped it would be Mexico, she told Jean, as she was longing to go to a Mexican church on Christmas Day.

From the start this family expedition was a success, to judge from Rose's letters, as well as from a series of snapshots which provide an interesting record of the trip. Rose looks full of zest, Will hearty and joking as ever, and Margaret happy and calm. It was an unsophisticated, out-of-doors holiday, an adventure that at times seems almost to have recaptured the gaiety of Varazze, even though all three of the participants were now in their late forties. What a different America Rose would have seen if she had gone there on a lecture tour, as she had recently thought of doing, staying in city after city, being lionised by culture-seekers, and everywhere encountering the effects of Prohibition, and the atmosphere of tension and anxiety – this was just after the Wall Street crash. But as it was, the Macaulays' travels kept them far from large cities, and in Rose's letters there is no mention of social or economic troubles, though political troubles did intrude at one point. When they reached the Mexican border, just after Christmas, the authorities looked askance at Margaret in her nun-like habit; the current régime in Mexico was anti-clerical and they refused to allow her into the country. There was no question of going on without her, so Rose's dreams of exploring Mexico and Guatemala came to nothing. She did however make a brief sortie across the frontier with Will, and was able to send Jean a photograph of herself stepping out briskly along a mountain trail as proof that she had set foot on Mexican soil. One cannot help smiling at Rose's appearance as she went striding along that mountain trail. Even in such a remote spot a townish hat was clamped on to her head, one of the cloche hats resembling tea cosies that were then in vogue.

After rejoining Margaret the party went on across the Californian desert and then through Arizona, New Mexico and southern Texas. Will's photographs give us glimpses of some of their stopping places; in one of the most dramatic, taken in Arizona, in the Gila desert, Rose is standing beside a giant cactus that towers above her. But these black and white photographs cannot of course convey the vividness of the scenery; for the colour we must turn to Rose's novel *Staying with Relations*, which was written immediately after her return home. In its final chapters the vast stretches of an American desert are the backdrop for an adventurous chase, by Essex car, in which the heroine (a young English novelist) and some of her friends are involved. But the plot and the characters fade into insignificance as Rose dwells upon the wild beauty of the landscape, lingering on its changing moods: *Staying with Relations* is indeed notable as the first of her books to display her gifts as a travel writer.

For the first time, too, in *Staying with Relations*, Rose gave her full attention to the automobile. She had had a driving licence since 1928, the year before the American trip, but her taste for adventurous motoring certainly dates from the expedition with Will and Margaret. There are some passages in *Staying with Relations* which obviously reflect Rose's own motoring experience. And there is also an admiring, almost affectionate tone in her accounts of the way in which the wretched Essex survived 'her' long series of ordeals and mishaps. 'The Essex plunged hub-deep through a wash, scrambled up a sharp grade beyond it, leaped some boulders, and sank profoundly into sand . . . It was a steep and rocky road, zigzagging over high grades; the surface, and particularly at each hairpin bend, seemed to have been prepared for a combination rockery and shingle beach . . . The Essex attempted to take in her stride some loose boulders for which her clearance was too low, scraped her bottom and jarred a spring. As they jolted, fortunately slowly, down the mountains . . . a rear wheel came off.' Soon after this the carburettor was spitting, 'having inadvertently absorbed some water from the washes they had traversed', and forty-two miles further on 'the radiator was found to be leaking at the rate of about a pint per mile'. At another point the road led through level country, 'dusty and gray-green with cactus and mesquite', where other cars, 'gaunt, wild, bone-shaking things, each filled to the teeth with swarthy [local] inhabitants . . . rattled by occasionally, enveloped in pale whorls of dust. Miles behind, miles ahead, they saw the dust-cloud that followed each car puffing along the road, as an engine is accompanied by its smoke. Often, in addition, there were clouds of steam. The Essex, too, every now and then threw up these, starting to boil like a kettle . . . In the hottest hour of the afternoon, they took off the radiator cap and the water spurted up like a geyser.'

From Texas, probably from Laredo, Rose went with Will for a second time a little way over the Mexican border, and this short excursion, along with the earlier one south of San Diego, comprised the total of her experience of Central America. Yet she had found it as stirring as she hoped she would. 'Mexico was wonderful', she wrote to Jean. 'I *do* wish we could have had longer there. If only they had let Margaret in, and if only the roads had been better. Still, we have been in it and seen it. My heart still pants after it.' This feeling of frustration haunted Rose and it was the impetus behind her choice of Guatemala as the setting for the first part of *Staying with Relations*. When a paperback edition of the novel was published in 1947 the blurb, presumably based on information supplied by Rose herself, stated that she had written the book 'largely as compensation for not having, in a tour of Central America, reached Guatemala and seen its ancient temples buried in Jungle'.

By the end of January 1930 the Macaulays had reached New Orleans. 'We got here', Rose told Jean, 'after a very interesting few days across the old negro sugar-plantation country. It is fascinating watching the changing panorama unwind itself, as if we were seeing a film. We left Spain behind us about three days ago, in Texas; ever since San Antonio the people in shops and restaurants and streets have stopped speaking Spanish and looking Mexican, and negroes abound everywhere instead, with their nice soft southern drawl . . . The Southern people are very frank about their attitude towards negroes – they say they can't help it, as they are Southerners . . . It is very queer in such nice kind people.'

'We left Spain behind us . . .' Yes, but the memory of it, and of the Spanish-speaking people of the South-West, remained with Rose and inspired some verses, 'Mexicans in California', which were published soon afterwards in a collection of contemporary English poetry.[1]

---

[1] *New English Poems: A Miscellany of Contemporary Verse never before published*, Edited by Lascelles Abercrombie (1931).

South and south of the redwood mountains,
    (Where the lumber rolls in rain)
South beyond the city of the Golden Gate,
    (Where the mist-blown streets climb steep, dip straight)
    You shall suddenly meet Spain.

All down the shores of the green Pacific
    The bastards of Cortes drift,
Lounge on the fishing-wharves of old Monterey,
Lade orange cargoes in San Diego bay,
    Trap turtle, and seek shrift.

On the hot wild slopes of old California,
    That was long since Mexico,
Lithe among the olives, the olive trees from Spain,
Blacker than their sires who sacked the Spanish main,
    Like mountain cats they go.

What turbulent blood from two fierce races
    Creeps in two black hot streams
Through the body and soul of the lithe dark man,
Through the blind dark soul of a Mexican,
    Coiled among stealthy dreams?

Behind and behind the Conquistadores
    And their arrogant, thieving bands,
There stretches a long brown lazy line –
Andalusians beneath the sun-scorched vine,
In Spanish posadas, drinking wine,
    Their quick knives in their hands.

But out from the heart of the whispering jungle
    And the desert's pale burnt gold,
Stalk stealthier breeds, with unswerving faces,
Stalk the Aztec, Maya, Apache races,
    And New Spain mates with old.

What stirs in your blood, you black-eyed greaser,
  With your mocking, ware-trap air?
What old-world, what new-world, devilries ride
On the beat of a pulse, on the surge of a tide,
  As you pitch ripe citrons there?

Some of the most charming of the photographs of Rose in
America were taken towards the end of the trip, when she and
Margaret and Will were in Florida. We see her sucking a coconut
beneath a tall palm tree, as usual in her tea-cosy hat, then posed
as a shipwrecked sailor, with a hand shading her eyes and 'scanning
the horizon for a sail'. We see her wading in the shallows off the
Florida Keys, bareheaded for once, in a bathing suit with a short
jacket over it, looking like a lanky curly-haired boy, while
beside her in the water is a small boat with Will at the oars. Years
later she gave an account of this last occasion in a broadcast talk:

We took a boat from one of the Keys – Key Largo by name –
and paddled about . . . landing on a mango-grown clump
of an island, and from there waded out into a sea shallow
enough to wade in knee-deep for an incredible way out.
The floor of the clear green water was grown with white
branch coral; and . . . among the coral darted the most
surprising little fishes, striped black and blue and coral red,
with the oddest faces and goggling eyes . . . I caught one of
them between my hands, and guided it to shore and put it in
a pool. But most of the fishes were too quick and slippery for
this, and all I could catch was coral. It was a lovely bathe,
with the clear green shallow Florida seas stretched for miles
round, glowing pink to the setting sun, and lapping with
little, shuffling whispers on the white sand of the palm-
fringed Keys. But it was a little too shallow; I mean, it was
more a paddle than a bathe.[1]

Rose had now been away from England for about two months.
'Our happiness is nearing its end, unluckily', she wrote to Jean,

[1] 'In Deep and Shallow Waters,' *The Listener*, 30 January 1936.

'but we must face facts, and neither money nor time will allow us very much longer.' By the end of February she was back in London, and a week or so later some of her friends gave a lunch party in Soho in her honour. Victor and Ruth Gollancz were there, and also Viola Garvin, Humbert Wolfe, and Roger Hinks, the art historian. This occasion is mentioned in a letter Hinks wrote to Naomi Royde-Smith (by now Mrs Ernest Milton) who was then herself in America, and it is well worth quoting as showing how Rose's simple holiday appeared to one of her sophisticated friends.

We assembled today at the Isola Bella, to welcome Rose on her return from America . . . As a matter of fact I had a foretaste of . . . [her] transatlantic experiences . . . on Saturday. The telephone bell rang, and, lifting the receiver, I heard the familiar staccato monologue. Characteristically she spent only two days in New York, and those while you were in Philadelphia. A pity, I think; I should like to have heard your impressions of each other against an unusual background. Rose ran on about coral strands and cactuses and what not; but you know how incoherent she is on the telephone . . . [She] seems to have returned unscathed. She looks very well, appears very cheerful, and is, I daresay, quite glad to be back among people who talk as fast as she does, instead of among the slow-tongued Americans. But . . . it still seems queer to me that people can cross the Atlantic twice and the North American Continent twice, endure New York, if only for two days – spend Christmas in Hollywood, motor through Mexico with their own hands, bathe at Palm Beach, and come back looking exactly the same as they did when they left.

Had Roger Hinks really feared that Rose would have picked up an American accent and an addiction to bootleg liquor? No. But he did not know her well enough to appreciate that when she came back to England she was not 'exactly the same as when she left'; she returned far less tense, far happier. During those two months with her brother and sister she had been really herself, leading one life instead of several. In some of the American photographs she looks not only cheerful and well but almost serene.

Rose's happiness was soon to bear fruits of a paradoxical kind. In *Staying with Relations* the main theme is a sombre one – the deceptive ambiguity of human character. As so often in her poetry, an undercurrent of melancholy and disillusion seems to have brought inspiration to Rose when she was at her most contented and relaxed. It was also at this time that her poetic impulse revived: 'Starting on poetry is like turning on a tap, with me. The trouble is to turn if off again', she wrote, shortly after this, to Victor Gollancz. Such then was her mood when she composed the following verses as an epigraph for *Staying with Relations*.

> Has the sea form? It breaks, it drifts,
>   Encountering with the steepy sands.
> Has water shape? It slips and shifts,
>   Thinner than dreams, between thy hands . . .
>
> Shifting as mist, men's secret selves
>   Slip like water, and drift like waves,
> Flow shadow-wise, and peer like elves
>   Mocking and strange, from the deep caves . . .
>
> Grasp at the wind; aye, bind the mist;
>   Read the bright riddling of the skies.
> But the soul, like slippery eel, will twist
>   Quick from thy clutch, and trick thine eyes

10

CAROLINE

THE ENGLISH SEVENTEENTH CENTURY had cast its spell over
Rose when she was an undergraduate, and ever since, when books
of the Caroline period came her way, she devoured them with
delight. Then in 1930 she was given the chance to concentrate
seriously on the works of some of the seventeenth-century
writers she loved: the Hogarth Press asked her to undertake a
short book for their series 'Lectures on Literature'. Her theme,
Some Religious Elements in English Literature, meant a survey of
the twelve centuries from Caedmon to Coventry Patmore, but
in the chapter on 'Anglican and Puritan' – the longest in the
book – she was able to dwell upon the writings of Donne, Milton,
Herrick, George Herbert, Henry Vaughan, Thomas Traherne,
Jeremy Taylor and Sir Thomas Browne.

This first attempt of Rose's at a scholarly work was completed
in March 1931, just before she went abroad for two months (to
Sicily with the Brookes, and then for a leisurely tour through
Italy). As she was leaving she wrote to Jean: 'My book is done,
after a desperate week of finishing it', and then she added, 'I now
want to write a life of Herrick ... The seventeenth century is so
very attractive.' Here then, in embryo, is Rose's initial impulse to
write the book which was to emerge the following year, not as a
biography, but as a historical novel centred upon Herrick: *They
Were Defeated*, the book which many people, including herself,
have thought the best she ever wrote.

The idea of a biography of a seventeenth-century poet was not however abortive. Soon after the publication of her book for the Hogarth Press Rose was asked to write a short life of Milton for Duckworth's series 'Great Lives'. In the resulting book, her next after *They Were Defeated*, Rose portrayed her 'great man' with what one enthusiastic reviewer called 'relentless, debunking wit', a treatment not to everyone's taste. Perhaps Milton was an unfortunate subject for Rose. Obviously his character was not nearly as congenial to her as Herrick's.

Why was she so much drawn to Robert Herrick? His poetry certainly enchanted her but there was more to it than that. For one thing his family and her own were distantly related (her father's paternal grandmother had been a Herrick) and there was also the more tenuous link that some of her Conybeare ancestors had lived in Devonshire, where for years Herrick was a country parson. But over and above this she was amused and fascinated by the poet's paradoxical personality. In *Some Religious Elements* she had claimed that he must be 'nearly the only seventeenth-century clergyman who continued to write love-poems and light odes after his ordination, and lightened the cares of his incumbency by maying-songs and uncivil lampoons upon the more irritating members of his flock.'

The next question is why Rose decided against a biography of Herrick in favour of a historical novel, a form so generally despised by the scholarly. One reason was that she was due to produce a new novel for Collins. But another, probably just as cogent, was that her imagination carried her away when she realised what possibilities would open up if Herrick, a Cambridge man, could be shown as visiting his old university just before the Civil War, and meeting the younger poets who were flourishing there at the time. Many years later, when asked how *They Were Defeated* came to her, Rose said that it developed from 'brooding on Cambridge life as it was about 1640... It was a lovely century in Cambridge; or anyhow those immediately pre-Civil-War years were. So much poetry, so much flowering of Anglicanism in the middle of Puritanism, so much idealism on both sides . . . I got a group of people, most of them real, some half real; I took Herrick and re-imagined him as a live person, how he would talk and feel; then I built up round him the Yarde family [they were Devonshire neighbours] and Dr Conybeare and Julian ["July", Dr Conybeare's fifteen-year-old daughter, herself a budding poet, was to be the book's tragic heroine] . . . Then I thought up the Cambridge milieu – and what fun it was! . . . Dr Conybeare . . . was the son of an Elizabethan schoolmaster who was my ancestor; we have the line of descent . . . I invented Dr Conybeare in a sense, but I made him as like as I could to my cousin Fred [Conybeare] of Oxford, atheism, appearance and all . . . I liked writing it, especially the part about Cambridge, which was very real to me, so were – and are – all the people in it.'[1]

When Rose embarked on 'Caroline', as she nicknamed her book, she resolved to aim at a standard of perfection not often attempted in historical novels; she would strive to use, in the talk of her characters, only words that she could identify as having been used in 1640 or thereabouts. One of her favourite hobbies was hunting down usages in her many-volumed Oxford Dictionary, nevertheless it was a *tour de force* that she achieved her purpose with only one or two slips. The worst of these, so she later discovered, was that she made someone speak of 'scientists' 'which no one really did till the nineteenth century; it should have been "philosophers".'

The few trifling errors in *They Were Defeated* did not detract from Rose's linguistic triumph; she entered so wholeheartedly into the spirit of the period – 'I . . . felt I was living in it' – that she succeeded in avoiding any impression of contrivance in her use of language. As one reviewer remarked: 'It is no laboured variation of current English that her characters use, but a vigorous native tongue as true to itself and its idiom as our everyday

[1] *Letters to a Friend,* pp. 27, 35, 299–300.

speech.'[1] And not only the dialogue shows this masterly touch; here and there in the narrative Rose slipped in a contemporary word or spelling, thereby seeming to take the reader into the mind and outlook of her seventeenth-century characters.

The first part of the book was set in Devonshire, and it was probably at the end of September 1931, soon after Rose's fiftieth birthday, that she made a visit to Herrick's parish, Dean Prior, a village just below south-east Dartmoor. And when we read of Julian Conybeare standing alone at the top of the lane above Deancombe village, we can picture Rose herself standing there, while 'the smoke of bonfires drifted sweetly on the light, cool air; behind her stretched the long dark gorge of the wood, climbing densely up Dean Bourne to the wild moors . . . She turned to where Deancombe lay huddled away in rosy orchards, beneath steep copses golden with furze, and beyond it to the south the blue landskip swelled and dipped. The day, the landskip, and the world, were so beautiful that they burned Julian's heart in her breast.'

But in *They Were Defeated* a dark, sinister side of the Devonshire scene is also in evidence. A witch hunt is afoot, and in the twilight, as Julian and her father walk through the quiet lanes, he tells her that he means to try and protect the local 'witch', old Moll Prowse. 'Oh father we must save her', urges Julian, and together the two rescue Moll. But the place where they hide her is soon discovered. In desperation Dr Conybeare saves her from torture and the stake by giving her a draught of poison.

After this, father and daughter leave Devonshire, and they make for Cambridge accompanied – in Rose's fancy – by Robert Herrick. To the eyes of the youthful Julian, poet and would-be scholar, the university town appears as 'a magical, enchanted city of towers and courts, philosophers and poets, lectures and books'. There is much of Rose herself in 'July', in her vulnerable tempera-

[1] Humbert Wolfe in *The Observer*, 16 October 1932.

ment, her romantic, poetic heart, her craving for learning, and her enjoyment of beauty and dignity in religious worship. In personal relations, too, there are parallels: July and one of her brothers are devoted companions; her hero-worship for Robert Herrick is somewhat comparable to Rose's adoring loyalty to her father, and when she is seduced by the masterful John Cleveland, and then forced to realise that her love for him involves contradictions, she suffers the same kind of turmoil that Rose herself endured. In physique July also resembled Rose; she had 'a child's form, undeveloped and straight', and like Rose she tended to blush. But the face of the lovely July was a typical Conybeare face, which Rose's was not.[1] Her looks are supposed to have been based on those of Dorothea Conybeare, who as a girl was very beautiful – 'a skin like lilies, eyes like pansies, a brow like alabaster'.

When Rose wrote *They Were Defeated* she had just changed flats. She had moved from St Andrew's Mansions to another smallish block near Marylebone Road called Luxborough House. Her new flat was an upstairs one, and in the summer of 1932 she wrote to Jean 'I sometimes feel no-one has a right to be so happy as I am in the flat, looking out on the trees on both sides, and so uninterrupted and comfortable and with my library all round me and my typewriter and pen ready to hand.'

Yet as the deadline for *They Were Defeated* approached she became discouraged and depressed, and confided to Jean that although she was 'getting on pretty well', she still had 'a lot of this unfortunate book to do'. 'What a lot of labour I have had over it, and how little anyone will care! I expect it will be a sad failure. But I have liked doing it; it is a consolation that one person has been interested.' This same point, that no one else was interested, is repeated in another letter to Jean, written when the book was at the proof stage. Jean and Margaret both read the

[1] R.M. took after the Fergusons, the family of her father's mother.

proofs and were eager in their praise, which heartened Rose considerably. 'One of my great comforts has been that you and M. both like my book – it is so important to my pleasure that the family should, even if no-one else does.' Evidently 'Caroline' had evoked apathy or disapproval in certain others. We can guess that Dorothy and Reeve Brooke, at this time two of Rose's closest friends, had not welcomed the 'serious' turn of her new book, for when she dedicated her next light novel, *Going Abroad*, to them, she added the words 'who desired a novel of unredeemed levity'. But a further implication of Rose's remarks to Jean, and an important one, is that *They Were Defeated* did not appeal to Gerald. Rose had, we know, come to count on him, more than anyone else, for advice and encouragement. So when she said to Jean 'no-one else' liked her historical novel, the critic uppermost in her mind must surely have been Gerald. And disparagement or mockery from him would amply account for her low spirits.

In the light of this, several episodes in Julian's story take on an added poignancy. When Cleveland, after becoming her lover, will have nothing of her intellectual enthusiasms, and with careless cruelty throws on to the fire the thesis that represents her most serious thinking, 'She was sharply, deeply hurt; she felt cold and bewildered with pain. What did he desire of her, then, if he did not desire her mind, her very self, all she cared for?... It was like a hard pebble flung at her heart.' Then later Cleveland is irked when July asks him to read her poetry. 'What does a lovely maid with rhyming, pray?' he mocks. 'It makes no differ, being a maid', Julian tells him, frowning and near to tears. 'When he spoke in this manner, her very heart seemed to weep... "It makes no differ. Men or women, if we crave to write verse, we must write it, and write it the best we can." For the first time in their intercourse, he turned from her impatiently, and she knew herself a bore in his laughing, quizzical eyes.' But she was trapped by her love. 'There *is* sadness in love. Always, Always,' she later reflects. 'For no two that love can feel alike in all things, and that hurts 'em. They'll desire different things, and think different thoughts, and love makes 'em give way though 'tis agen their reason and their wishes, for they desire love more than all else. They must renounce being themselves and lay by their wills, and deny their whole lives, just for love. 'Tis what Dr Donne and Mr Herbert and St Thomas à Kempis and all great Christians else have said of religion, that we must deny all for't and lay down our very lives. And so 'tis with love.'

They Were Defeated, when it was published in October 1932, had a mixed reception and sold less well than Rose's novels usually did (the American edition, renamed *The Shadow Flies*, failed to earn its advance). But perhaps this was only to be expected. In the words of the *Times Literary Supplement*'s reviewer 'The public is conservative and inclined to demand from its favourites that to which it is used.' By a few, however, a discriminating few, the book was received with rapture. Humbert Wolfe, finding his hopes for Rose as a writer fulfilled at last, contributed a long review to Viola Garvin's literary pages in *The Observer*, under the heading 'Another Macaulay – Historian'.

> To the great enrichment of English letters Miss Macaulay has . . . chosen a historical subject. Those acquainted with her curious erudition, as well as with the sap of knowledge in her blood derived from so many distinguished ancestors, will not expect a cloak-and-dagger romance. They will look rather for a new *John Inglesant* or even an *Héloïse and Abélard*. They will anticipate that, whatever the period, Miss Macaulay will make it populous with living men and women, wisely, drily and most pertinently observed. They will not be disappointed . . . In many ways *They Were Defeated* is a new departure for Miss Macaulay, because for the first time she has used all her powers both of poet and novelist . . . As a result she has achieved her greatest success.

They Were Defeated left Rose so steeped in the seventeenth century that when, after polishing off her Milton biography and then *Going Abroad*, she decided to try something new, an anthology, she naturally tended to fasten upon writings of the same period. Collecting the material for her book *The Minor Pleasures of Life* was thus an enjoyable task, though it meant interminable searching and transcribing; when, after many cuts, the book was published by Gollancz in 1934 it contained more than 700 pages.

Some of the 'minor pleasures' that Rose selected were characteristically her own: Bathing, Conversation, Exercise, Sermons, The Single Life; but she also included many which she herself did not share. In the section headed 'Female Pleasures', for instance, the first item (which must be given here in full, for reasons that will presently emerge) was on the subject of Hunting. It was a poem entitled 'The Chase', whose authorship Rose gave as 'Anon', with the date 'c. 1675'.

Thro' the green Oake-wood on a lucent Morn
Turn'd the sweet mazes of a silver Horn:
A Stag rac'd past, and hallowing hard behind,
Dian's young Nymphs ran fleeting down the Wind.
A light-foot Host, green-kirtl'd all they came,
And leapt, and rollickt, as some mountain Streame
Sings cold and ruffling thro' the Forrest Glades;
So ran, so sang, so hoyted the Moone's Maids.
Light as young Lev'retts skip their buskin'd feet,
Spurning th'enamell'd Sward as they did fleet.
The Wind that buss'd their cheekes was all the Kiss
Was suffer'd by the Girles of *Artemis*,
Whose traffique was in Woods, whom the wing'd Boy
Leauguer'd in vain, whom Man would ne're injoy,
Whose Bed greene Moss beneath the forrest Tree,
Whose jolly Pleasure all in Liberty,

To sport with fellow Maids in maiden cheere,
To swim the Brook, and hollo after Deer.
Thus, the winds wantoning their flying Curles,
So rac'd, so chas'd, those most Delightfull Girles.

Ten years later, in 1944, this poem proved an embarrassment to Rose, for when the eminent bibliophile John Hayward was preparing a collection of seventeenth-century verse, he asked her to specify its source. 'Unfortunately you happened on the only thing in that book which is not quite as it seems,' she replied. 'The fact is that I wanted a poem about women hunting and couldn't lay my hands on one at the moment, so I thought I would write one myself, and it amused me to put it into 17th-century garb and date it "c. 1675". (After all, how many years may *circa* cover? I thought perhaps 260 years or so) . . . It wasn't meant as a leg-pull, only as a private experiment of my own. As a matter of fact I have written a fair amount of pseudo-period verse; it is, as perhaps you know yourself, a rather entertaining pastime. One can take some modern poem and rewrite it in the style of each century, or perhaps one should say of each decade or so. It might be a good parlour game for those whom it amuses.'

John Hayward evidently entered into the spirit of Rose's 'private experiment'. 'Thank you so much for a very charming and nice letter', she wrote again to him. 'I think you are right as to the too late dating of my piece; the spirit is earlier; but if I had put it much earlier, I should have made some of the spelling and capital letters a little different. What I felt, and feel, dubious about is the rhyming of girl with curl. Did Pope do it, or any 18th century poet? Or 17th century? By the eighteenth century they were pronouncing it gal, or gairl, I suppose – how much earlier I don't know. And it wasn't a good 19th century rhyme. My parents always reprimanded us if we said "gurl"; now it is usual, in the last twenty years or so, I think. Still, I dare say 17th century rhymesters weren't so very particular always.'

The Minor Pleasures of Life was soon followed by a companion volume, *Personal Pleasures*, this time not an anthology but a series of short essays on some of the pleasures that had brought enjoyment to Rose herself. Once again her aptitude for archaic English was much in evidence. 'What a mass of learning you are! And particularly of Elizabethan and Jacobean learning!' Gilbert Murray commented some years later, when she gave him a copy of the book. 'It is a quality rarely combined with so much wit and impudence. And how you are in love with the mere art of language. It is your sentences and turns of phrase that give the book such a character of its own.'

With her heart more and more in the seventeenth century and its semantics, the churning out of the topical novels that were expected of her became increasingly a burden for Rose, with results that could not be hidden from the perceptive. *Going Abroad*, which was published two years after *They Were Defeated*, was a skit on the Oxford Group which drew plenty of laughs.[1] But it also drew some scathing criticisms, such as the following from the *New Statesman*'s reviewer:[2] 'A humorous view of life, whether inherent or adopted for the purposes of writing a "holiday" novel, defeats its object . . . Humour must be a by-product of either profound or vivid interest in persons and events, however much this interest be clothed in levity. The impression is made that Miss Macaulay is amused by, but not deeply interested in, people.' What a gulf existed between Rose's two styles! In the context of *They Were Defeated* this last remark would have been unthinkable.

The deterioration in Rose's light fiction was even more evident

[1] After it was out R.M. realised that she had wounded the feelings of various 'Oxford Groupers' and had qualms of conscience. In 1950, writing to Father Johnson, she admitted that she wished she had not written the book. 'One shouldn't make fun of people who . . . are after all on the right side as between moral good and evil.'

[2] The review was unsigned.

in her next novel, *I Would be Private*, a fanciful satire on the predicament of a young policeman and his wife who become the parents of quintuplets; when it appeared three years later, in 1937, even Humbert Wolfe had to admit that it was 'one of her slightest'. And as to sales, a letter from Rose's publisher, W. A. R. Collins, to her agent Spencer Curtis Brown, written a little time after the book was out, throws searching light upon this stage of Rose's career as a novelist. Her last contract with Collins had apparently dated from 1929, 'a time when Miss Macaulay was writing novels regularly at two-yearly intervals and when her sales were steady in the neighbourhood of 15,000 . . . There have, however, been longer and longer intervals between each of Miss Macaulay's novels, as she has been spending much of her time in doing other work, and . . . she [has] kept finding it difficult to think out plots for new novels. One of the results of the long intervals between her books and of her difficulties over plots has been that her sales have suffered a very considerable drop. *I Would be Private* sold just over 8,000 copies . . . in the original (Home) edition, representing a drop of almost 50%, and leaving us with an unearned royalty of £465, a considerable loss on any book.'

Here a word may be added on the state of Rose's overall financial situation. It seems that since *Potterism* she had lived mainly on the proceeds of her writings, and the decline in her fiction in the 1930s would have been a serious matter if her private resources had not been augmented at this time. But after 1937, when Regi Macaulay died, her income from investments increased in a spectacular manner. Henceforth, for the rest of her life, she was comfortably off irrespective of royalties.[1]

The diverging of the mainstream of Rose's creative impulse from light fiction to writings of greater depth may have been one of the

---

[1] By 1950 her gross private income had reached the neighbourhood of £1,500 per annum; by 1958 it was over £3,500. After her death it was

reasons why she developed, during the 1930s, a strong dislike for any publicity about herself, especially about herself as a novelist. And it was from now on that she tried to suppress her earliest novels. This is well illustrated by some letters she wrote to Frank Swinnerton in 1934. He had asked if he could include extracts from her writings in his book *The Georgian Literary Scene*. Rose replied that he might but added, 'I can only ask you, not as a right, but in appeal to your charity, not to quote anything too jejune and adolescent.' When she learnt that he wanted to use something from *Abbots Verney* she was horrified. 'Oh dear, oh dear', she wrote back. 'Must you really quote from that absurd, juvenile, and (I hope) forgotten book?... I do rather wish you wouldn't. I've written such lots since, that I don't mind people reading. Couldn't you quote instead from *Orphan Island*, or *A Casual Commentary* (much more characteristic) or *Mystery at Geneva* or *They Were Defeated* ... or, indeed, anything written in my more adult days?'

She was also dismayed to hear that he planned to include a section on herself in his chapter on the younger Georgian novelists, along with writers such as Compton Mackenzie, Hugh Walpole and Mary Webb. 'Must there be a section about me?' she pleaded. 'If you knew how I hate being written about, even by the nicest critics – except just in reviews of my books as they come out ... You see, I never feel like a novelist at all, and would much rather only my essays, or literary books, or even verse, were discussed ... I think my own novels so bad (as novels) that no-one could think them worse. All I am interested in when I write them is the style – the mere English, the cadences etc; and sometimes when I make a joke. As stories, and as characterisations, they bore me to death. So will you consent to leave me out of your discussion of novelists? You would be very kind and

announced, to the amazement of many of her friends, who were accustomed to her frugal ways, that she had left £84,085 (duty paid £37,959).

obliging if you would, and I should always remember it in your favour . . . Forgive my being so troublesome; I suppose I have a tiresome fad about this, and feel stupidly shy; but there it is!'[1]

With regret Swinnerton bowed to Rose's insistence and left out some of the 'illuminating extracts' he had hoped to quote. But fortunately he did not cut his section on Rose Macaulay the novelist – it is a shrewd and percipient sketch.

[1] Another sidelight on R.M.'s feelings about her own novels, written not long after this (on 7 June 1938) occurs in a letter to Daniel George: 'I never dare to read my novels once they are published, so I simply don't know what they are like. Perhaps when I am very old I shall dare, and shall feel no more responsibility for them . . . Till then I shall refrain.'

II

SPEED ADDICT

'I LOVE driving my car!' So Rose exclaimed, with all the exultation of a newly-fledged owner-driver, in a letter written in the summer of 1934. This was when she was writing *Personal Pleasures*, and no less than three of the most enthusiastic essays in the book concern motoring and possessing a car. The first of them, 'Driving a Car', tells of Rose's feelings as she discovered that on the open road she could savour a sense of freedom and power as well as the physical thrill of speed.

To devour the flying miles, to triumph over roads, flinging them behind us like discarded snakes, to rush . . . from morn to noon, from noon to dewy eve, a summer's day, up hill and down, by singing fir woods and blue heath, annihilating counties and minifying kingdoms – here is a joy . . . With open throttle and hands lightly on the wheel we scud the roads, watching the needle mount . . . All is bliss; we hum songs of triumph . . . Our song is chorused by the little chirping squeak of the door handles, the faint rattling of the windows, the less faint humming of the engine, the running of the wind. The scenery is doubled in charm by being seen at this rate; it flashes by with the vividness of a string of jewels, glimpsed, admired and gone.

But even in the 1930s there was a 'traffic problem'. 'The serpent in this Eden, the canker in this lovely bloom of speed, is (need one say it?) the other vehicles in our road. And particularly in the middle of our road which is where cars, horse-carts and cyclists love to travel.'

Rose seldom tried to conceal her joyful egotism as a driver; at times she even boasted of it. In *Personal Pleasures* she described how after finding on her car an advertiser's slogan 'Fastest on Earth' she cherished the label, and dreamt of keeping it prominently displayed so that other cars – buses even – might yield to her Morris 'in the Hyde Park Corner scuffle, at the Marble Arch roundabout, and dashing up Baker Street. "There goes", they should say, "the Atalanta among cars; see how it swifts along, passing all others; it travels post, it shoots through space like a star, or would, were it not held up by other traffic and by policemen; it is the car of Mercury himself, make way, make way!" ' The very thought of going thus 'tagged and bragged' so she declared 'intoxicates, weights my foot on the accelerator, speeds my swift course around St James's Square.'

The third of Rose's motoring Pleasures was 'Talking about a New Car', and this essay too reflected her own experience: much as she loved her first car it was already ancient when she bought it, and was soon showing its age.

Yes, the time has come. The two low gears make a noise like the large cats at the Zoo at lunch-time, and even top is like the large cats purring *after* lunch, or like an aeroplane zooming just overhead. I must have a car which makes noises like small cats purring in their sleep, or, at worst, like an aeroplane a thousand feet up. Besides, the thing takes so long to pick up speed. And it groans. And drinks petrol like a fish. And it can't get up Primrose Hill on second now.

So, after about a year, Rose changed her car for another second-hand Morris which was 'only a year old', so she told Jean, 'and with very little use before I had it; it is rather smaller than the other (10 h.p.) and handier, and goes much more quietly (I mean, makes less noise). I like it very much. Having a new car should have been one of my Pleasures. The temptation is to drive about all day and do no work.'

In a succession of cars, throughout the remainder of her life, Rose continued to drive about, with unflagging gusto and in a carefree and dangerous manner. Victor Gollancz has told of her arrival for a weekend at Brimpton 'with one of her mudguards hugging the ground; a cow had sat on it, she said'.[1] *Why*, one may ask, did Rose drive like this? Was lack of attention chiefly to blame for her petrifying performances at the wheel? Often it was, but there were other reasons besides. For one thing she relished the kick of danger. Ever since Varazze, when she had ridden the spirited pony, Pinz, she had lived up to the family motto *Dulce Periculum* far more than any of her brothers and sisters. Towards the end of her life, when she bragged to a friend (Frank Singleton) about what she called the most daring exploit of her motoring career, 'twisting down single-track Mexican mountains', it was obviously an enjoyable memory to her. Another pertinent fact is that Rose never took any formal driving lessons; before 1935 driving tests were not compulsory in England, and so far as Jean can remember Rose 'taught herself'. Also, of course, during her gruelling initiation as a driver – her American trip – she had become used to driving on the right-hand side of the road.

So far as the nerves of her friends were concerned, Rose had something of a blind spot, and many stories have been told of hair-raising incidents. Compton Mackenzie tells in his autobiography (*Octave Eight*) how in the 1930s Rose gave him a lift after they had been fellow guests at a lunch party.

As we drove round Regent's Park in a series of wide sweeps the drivers of other cars were shaking angry fists at Rose

[1] During the 1930s R.M. frequently weekended with the Gollanczs at Brimpton in Berkshire; usually the Lynds were also there, and often the Brookes, the David Lows and Humbert Wolfe (*Reminiscences of Affection*, pp. 75, 85).

and pedestrians were leaping in a panic to the pavement . . .

'Stop, Rose.'

'Stop?'

'Yes, I want to get out.'

'Don't you want to hear the end of the story I was telling you?'

'I shall probably always regret not hearing the end of it, but the flesh is weak. Please stop and let me get out.'

'You won't find a taxi.'

'I shall walk to Baker Street.'

She stopped on the wrong side of the road as I hastily got out. I see now Rose Macaulay sweeping on southward in a series of ample zig-zags.

As a child Rose had longed to fly; so had her brothers and sisters. Whenever they saw a new moon, so Jean remembers, they used to murmur 'I wish I could fly'. So it was appropriate that Rose's first flight took place in the company of two of her sisters, Margaret and Eleanor. In January 1932 Eleanor was on leave, and it was her idea that they should go for a joyride from one of the aerodromes near London (we do not know which). The flight, so Rose told Jean afterwards, was a 'thrilling experience'. But it was also very nearly a humiliation. 'It was rather bumpy, and Margaret all but succumbed, and I felt a qualm or two . . . The aerodrome man said it was a bad afternoon for it, so we felt proud of having stuck it out.'

Two or three years later Rose went up again, this time from Heston with one of her publisher friends, Hamish Hamilton, who was a keen pilot. He took her up in a Klemm monoplane, an open low-wing machine (it had only one magneto and no certificate of airworthiness – facts of which Rose was unaware). While she was being strapped in she joked about reaching the ground first if they looped the loop. The passenger's seat had a stick and after a while Rose was allowed to take over. Hamish

Hamilton can still remember what happened when he told her to push the stick forward. 'Usually when I told my passengers to do this and we started to move rapidly towards the earth they would scream. Not Rose. She merely did what she was told, banking steeply as well, and enjoyed every moment of it.' He also recalls the following incident during the flight: 'The telephone connecting the pilot's seat with that of the passenger was never particularly effective, and Rose's rapid and not very clear diction didn't help matters. Accordingly when she asked me an urgent but inaudible question I landed and said "What *were* you saying, Rose?". "I was asking," she replied, "if you could make it stand still in the air." '

After this flight from Heston Rose wrote an essay on flying which she included in *Personal Pleasures*. In it she told of the 'enormous bliss' of speeding 'through radiant space'. This subsequently gave rise to the quite untrue legend that Rose herself became a pilot. Later on she made use of air transport whenever convenient, but she never thought of learning to fly herself, which was perhaps just as well. As Raymond Mortimer has written, 'Thank goodness, one lesson in flying seems to have been enough for her . . . The notion of being her passenger in the air turns me to gooseflesh.'

Every week during the first eight months of 1935, and then intermittently until the end of the following year, Rose wrote a column for *The Spectator* called 'Marginal Comments'; altogether she produced sixty-two of them. Each week she took some news item that had caught her fancy or some subject of topical interest, and dashed off half a page of lively chat in rather the same dry, mocking style, peppered with seventeenth-century terms and allusions, that she had used in *Personal Pleasures*. No one kind of subject was dominant. But whenever 'the traffic problem' was freshly in the news she was sure to discuss it, and in several of her pieces she castigated dangerous drivers. One such piece which included strong comment on a recent trial, involved her and *The Spectator*, early in 1936, in serious trouble.

The trial had been an unusual one. A young peer, Lord de Clifford, had been charged with dangerous driving and manslaughter after a crash on the Kingston by-pass in which the driver of the other car was killed. The fact that the defendant was a peer, and that manslaughter was technically a felony, meant that the manslaughter charge had to be brought against him in the House of Lords. When the trial 'by his peers' took place, with traditional pomp, Lord de Clifford was acquitted, and his further acquittal (in the Central Criminal Court) on the dangerous driving charge was little more than a formality. Rose was scandalised. She disapproved on principle of elaborate ceremonial, and to Jean she wrote, 'I quite agree with you about Lord de Clifford's trial. A disgusting exhibition, and *so* expensive. And what did his counsel mean by saying that driving on the wrong side of the road was no proof of negligence? It seems to me one of the most negligent things a motorist can do.'

The second acquittal, at the Old Bailey, on top of all the fuss at the House of Lords, spurred Rose to air her views in *The Spectator*:

After a parade of mummery and pantomime which seems to be the fault of no one but the law of the land, the defendant is acquitted on both charges, without even a suspended or an endorsed licence. It would appear that driving on the wrong side of the road is considered by the law less dangerous than other motoring crimes . . . less so, for example, than taking a corner too fast, for which a woman last year received a sentence of nine months . . . Selfish drivers continually drive on the crown, or over the crown, of the road . . . it is a common sin. Lord de Clifford's counsel said, at the House of Lords trial, that it was no evidence of negligence; possibly it is more often evidence of reckless selfishness, stupidity and bad manners . . . The laws by which motoring offences are tried certainly seem to be in a state of confusion only matched by the traffic chaos itself . . . Still, it does seem clear that to drive on the wrong side of the road cannot be right.

Lord de Clifford, very understandably, was offended by Rose's remarks, and brought an action for libel against her and *The Spectator*. On 10 March a settlement in his favour was announced, and a disparaging phrase used by the Lord Chief Justice (the late Lord Hewart), 'It is a disgraceful libel', was of course pounced on by the Press. To a friend Rose wrote: 'Did you read the report of our libel case? We made a withdrawal in court, and settled for £600 . . . Fortunately the *Spectator* paid it all, so I only shall have my own costs to pay – heavy enough, God wots. The Lord Chief Justice . . . went out of his way to stigmatize my very gentle-manly libel (*entirely* about off-side driving) . . . trying to make out that it had been scurrilous comments on the private life of . . . [Lord de Clifford]. The *Spectator* and I, both so respectable, are very angry with him . . . You would find my libel very dull, in spite of the Lord Chief's efforts to make it seem spicy.'

Only two days after this High Court case, Rose herself had to appear at the Marlborough Street police court for a motoring offence; she had been summonsed for 'obstructing', i.e. leaving her car too long in the street. It was her first offence and she was fined thirty shillings. We cannot be sure whether on this occasion she gave her name as 'Emily Macaulay'. Later she habitually did so to avoid publicity when charged with driving and parking offences.

Her afternoon at Marlborough Street did much to mollify her opinion of the Law, and she wrote glowingly of police courts and magistrates in 'Marginal Comments' the following week. She also at this time acquired a sincere respect for the London police; perhaps this was why the hero of her next novel, *I would be Private*, was a policeman. The book included several echoes of her recent brushes with the Law, and she even went so far as to introduce an episode very similar, in some respects, to the de

Clifford case; the hero resigns from the Police Force when his superiors disregard his report on a fatal motor accident and hush up the case because a celebrity is incriminated.

In this context Rose expressed some interesting views on road accidents. When her hero goes off abroad to start a new life, the fact that he had been involved in 'a case' is mentioned to a local vicar. 'What case?' the vicar asks. 'An unjust case, about a car and an M.P. or something.' 'And the vicar thought that would be all right', Rose continued, 'so long as a car was in it; there is something less unpleasant about the iniquities committed by these terrific and ravening machines than about some of those perpetrated by humanity outside them. Cars are like wild animals, tigers and so on; or like war; they assault and devour people, and it is all very callous and selfish and dreadful, but there is a difference – one does not shrink back in disgust and desire that one's daughters should not know about it.'

12

PEACE OR WAR?

FOR QUITE A WHILE, as the skies over Europe darkened, Rose's attitude towards the international scene remained aloof and amused; neither Mussolini or Hitler alarmed her, nor did she take their ideologies seriously. She treated politics, whether at home or abroad, as absurd and highly diverting, although she liked to regard herself as a faithful Liberal. She had always supported the League of Nations, and when Abyssinia was invaded she was torn between disapproval and her love for Italy. But Mussolini made an excellent scapegoat. 'Will suggests that everyone should draw lots, and the shortest would have to shoot the Duce', she wrote to Jean. 'I quite agree. It would be a noble death for the assassin. I *do* wish some one would; I don't believe anything else can now stop this business. Do you think I ought to go out and have a try, as I feel so strongly about it? I don't feel it would disgrace the family name, but rather honour it.' Two months later she was still writing in the same vein. 'I feel Abyssinia is abandoned to her fate. Sanctions will do no good at this date, and the Italian army seems to be strolling unopposed over the land (fortunately). If there is no more bloodshed than this, it won't be too bad a war. I suppose Italy will be allowed to settle there in peace. It is all very, very wicked, but I hope the climate won't suit them and they will get tired of it soon.'

To Rose the avoidance of bloodshed was the thing that mattered supremely. And it was partly this that in time, when the Spanish war was looming, drew her towards pacifism. But only partly; the main reason was 'Dick' Sheppard. Before she met him she had not liked what she knew of him – he had 'too facile an approach and too popular an appeal'.[1] But at their first meeting she was won over by his friendliness and sense of humour. His quick repartee was well matched with her own, and a conversation between the two has been likened to a game of squash rackets. Sheppard possessed some of the same qualities that had long ago attracted her to Father Waggett; though far less brainy he had the same sort of warmth and sparkle.

In June 1936 Rose agreed to be a 'sponsor' for Sheppard's Peace Pledge Union, which meant that she would speak in public and write to the Press: other sponsors were Charles Raven, Donald Soper, Ellen Wilkinson and Storm Jameson. Yet at heart she was unconvinced, for she doubted whether pacifism would work. She was easily swayed, too, by adverse criticisms. That October, after hearing Gilbert Murray speak on the need for armaments to keep the peace, she wrote to him, 'I always doubt if it is wise for those who may differ from you even slightly to hear you speak, as they stand in grave risk of having their minds changed! Mine is, on armaments, so wavering anyhow, that it is particularly in danger; and all the time you spoke, I was agreeing . . . I am haunted by your saying that you thought the advocates of complete pacifism here were doing harm; it is a fearful thought, that I often have.'

The vacillating nature of Rose's pacifism is clear from an apologia that she wrote, *An Open Letter to a Non-Pacifist*; it was published as a pamphlet in 1937. She set out to explain what pacifism is, but only succeeded in demonstrating that there are many contradictory variants of it; she also showed that most pacifists, including herself, were themselves inconsistent.

Speaking for myself, if some one were to attack and try to rob or injure me, or if I saw him attacking some weaker person, I should endeavour by all means (though probably unsuccessfully) to knock him down. But mass passive

[1] See *Dick Sheppard and his Friends* (1938).

resistance against mass aggression or tyranny is certainly a pacifist doctrine.

Her final summing up was hardly less tentative:

The situation seems urgent. For if civilization, even such as it is, is to go under in hatred and lies, blown to bits by crashing hordes of bombing planes, as it is even now being blown to bits in Spain, it is going to be pretty difficult to put the pieces together again . . . Culture will be gone, barbarism will reign, the clock will have swung back through the centuries to a darker age, because not enough people would reject the conventions of contemporary warfare as too cruel, too horrible, for civilized humanity to accept as a conceivable method of settling differences with one another.

Although Rose's pacifism was in some ways so superficial it had strong emotional roots. For it stemmed from a revulsion against violence and cruelty, and from her acute sensitivity to pain. Yet even here there was a contradiction, for in spite of the horror that physical suffering kindled in her she was not altogether anti-military; there was still in her something of the young hero-worshipper who had relished tales of daring, and had herself longed to be a man.

In October 1937 Sheppard stood as Peace Pledge Union candidate for the Rectorship of Glasgow University, and Rose volunteered to speak for him. On arriving at the Central Station she found herself plunged into the atmosphere of an under-graduate rag, and she was very nearly kidnapped by the supporters of one of Sheppard's rivals, a Scottish Nationalist. They were scheming to make off with her to some secret hiding place until the election was over. Pretending to be Pacifists they inveigled her into their car, and she was rescued only just in time by the *bona fide* Pacifists amidst a barrage of paper missiles.

The election resulted in an easy victory for Sheppard, not only over the Scottish Nationalist but over two further rivals, Professor J. B. S. Haldane and Winston Churchill. It was a short-lived triumph. On 31 October, just before Sheppard was to give his inaugural address, he suffered a fatal heart attack. His death came as a profound shock to Rose. 'When Dick Sheppard died', she wrote in *Peace News*, 'the world's temperature seemed to drop, so much did he raise and warm it . . . Max Beerbohm once said to me of him "When he comes into a room everyone feels happier and comes more alive" . . . As to his cause, one can hear him using General Wolfe's dying words to his soldiers before Quebec: "The day is ours, keep it." The day is not yet ours; nor will it be, one surmises, in this generation, but Dick was a hoper.'

Rose herself was less of a hoper. Within a few months of Sheppard's death her allegiance to the pacifist cause broke down. She still took an interest in the Peace Pledge Union, but in March 1938, while the Nazi armies were sweeping into Austria, she resigned her sponsorship.

Just at the time of Dick Sheppard's death a project was launched which was to focus Rose's thoughts on the problems of pacifism from a new angle. An organisation called the International Peace Campaign suggested that she should compile an anthology on the subject of man's varying attitudes towards peace and war. She could not have undertaken it single-handed, for she was busy with a new study for the Hogarth Press, *The Writings of E. M. Forster* (her first book of contemporary literary criticism), but she was glad to share the work with an experienced anthologist, Daniel George.[1] This partnership was to prove felicitous, for he delighted in the archaic and the dryly humorous, the whimsical and the abstruse, and in the course of his collaboration with Rose they became firm friends. Subsequently, too, they continued to correspond fairly steadily; his heartfelt admiration for her meant that he was only too glad to act as her researcher and literary helper whenever further chances occurred.

The work of hunting down material for the 'peace anthology',

[1] Daniel George Bunting (1890–1967).

which they called *All in a Maze*, was done almost entirely by
Daniel George, while Rose advised on the selections and wrote
an Introduction. Most of the excerpts were poetic heart-cries
and protests against the horrors of war, but to try and give a
balanced picture they also included a few martial items such as a
passage from a poem called *Il Bellicoso* beginning 'Hence, dull
lethargic Peace'. Then at the last minute they decided to add, in
the final section, quite a number of press reports and editorials,
mainly from *The Times*, concerning the events which had just
culminated in the Munich Agreement. Later Rose regretted this.
The book was not a success, and although doubtless the main
reason was its propagandist tone, a chief target for complaints
was the press-cutting finale. 'Of the earlier part, I hear nothing
but good', Rose wrote to her fellow-editor, trying to console
him, '[but] some people find the end part too full of Chamberlain
and *The Times*, and think that gives it a pro-Munich bias, which
is rather the feeling I have myself.' She said she now wished they
had given more prominence to the view of 'those who think that
even war is not so dreadful and wrong as letting people be bullied
and enslaved'.

The multitudinous letters and postcards Rose wrote to Daniel
George were not altogether confined to their literary interests.
Every now and then she would add some comment on the news
of the day, and behind the banter there are valuable clues as to the
evolution of her thinking. Just before Munich she had been
abroad, spending part of her holiday at Varazze, and basking in
the euphoria that Italy always induced. And on the very day when
Chamberlain first met Hitler at Berchtesgaden she wrote to
Daniel George: 'I am lotus-eating (or rather fig and peach-eating)
in this Eden, in a blue warm sea or on sweet-smelling hills. Every
one charming. I read the oddest news in the local press! But I eat
another fig and forget it. It seems that the poor Sudetici are being
practically all massacred by the dreadful "Cechi". But Varazze
doesn't much care.' Later on the same day she wrote again: 'Our

P.M. seems to have saved the world! Even the Italian press is loud in acclamation – 69, and never set foot in the air before (they say). If war is so easily averted as all this, it does seem a pity no P.M. ever thought of it before. I gather from my *Corriere* that Londoners have quite lost their heads, and stand all day and night in Whitehall and Downing Street as if there was a motor-crash to watch. The *Corriere* rather admires this. I'm glad I am out of the hysteria. In Varazze we are very placid and gay, and I don't think we know what a Crisis it all is, or quite who these Sudetici and Cechi are. I hope today's great interview was a success; as I get no evening news I shan't know till tomorrow.' A week later, when Chamberlain was again meeting Hitler, at Godesberg, Rose had gone on to the Basque country, and from St Jean de Luz she wrote: 'Yes, Peace without Honour seems to be what we've got. I'm glad. One can't expect *both*.'

Six months later however, when Hitler's seizure of Czechoslovakia showed that he had no intention of abiding by the Munich Agreement, Rose was in a very different frame of mind, and when she wrote to her old friend Edward Marsh to congratulate him on his memoirs, she expressed a new-found pessimism: 'It is a lovely and rich tapestry you have woven, and sad, of course, because one feels that kind of rich and happy life and culture poised now over a dark and terrifying abyss.' In March 1939 she decided to take definite action so as to be prepared for war. There was much talk of plans for the evacuation of civilians from London, and she was determined not to be banished to the country against her will. So she joined the London Auxiliary Ambulance Service as a volunteer part-time driver. Despite her erratic driving she had a clean licence and had never been involved in an accident.

But her newly realistic attitude did not prevent her from cracking jokes as usual with Daniel George about the danger-signals in Europe. When Italy invaded Albania in April she wrote: 'I find now that I am quite inured to the week-end coups of dictators, and the swallowing of Albania scarcely makes me look up from my books. Are you the same? We are being trained up – or down. The journalists seem to be able to turn on the same indignation each time. But Hitler produced, I think, his best remark yet, about Italy's deep sympathy with the Albanians. I could almost like the fellow, if I thought he enjoyed his own *mots* – but I fear he doesn't.' Then a few weeks later, when Conscription was announced, and she learnt that Daniel George's son John was in the age-group concerned, she was full of sympathy, though still apparently hopeful that Britain could avoid war. 'Bad luck . . . I'm sorry your son is due for this nonsense . . . But I don't think our government means anything by its pledge [to guarantee Poland], does it? Two can double-cross, if it comes to that. I don't see "Gallant little Poland" ever being a British battle cry.'

The Nazi threat had little immediacy for Rose until almost the brink of war, and even then she remained baffled. When she heard rumours in the late spring of 1939 that *Peace News* (to which she still sometimes contributed) was coming under the influence of Nazi propagandists all she could do was to lash out blindly: 'Yes, d - - - the Nazis. They are persecuting us all, befuddling our minds and dominating our imaginations and making pacifism impossibly difficult. I hate it.'

Rose's literary partnership with Daniel George did not end when *All in a Maze* went to press, for a new subject, 'Animals in Literature', had already captured her imagination, and he needed no urging to continue looking out material for her. We do not know what first inspired her to compose the modern equivalent of a bestiary, but some years earlier she had enjoyed reviewing an English edition of La Fontaine's fables (translated by Edward Marsh) and this may have had something to do with it. Soon she was accumulating a mass of intriguing animal lore, such as some references to the loves of dolphins and turtles (she was puzzled to know why Spenser thought the turtle chooses 'her' dear, while other creatures choose 'his'). But much as she would have liked to start immediately on her 'Animal book' she could no longer postpone a new novel for Collins; it was now two years since *I would be Private*. So although batches of exciting finds poured in from Daniel George she set them aside and gradually, laboriously, a new novel – a sombre, groping book – began to take shape. Its setting was war-ravaged Spain, and its title was a despairing one, *And No Man's Wit*, taken from Donne's poem 'An Anatomie of the World':

> The Sun is lost, and the earth, and no man's wit
> Can well direct him where to looke for it.

The story centres around the wanderings of an incongruously assorted party from England, the family and friends of a young man with Communist leanings who has been reported missing with the International Brigade. His mother, a busybody with strong Liberal views, leads the search for her lost son. Rose's portrayal of this lady's progress through Franco Spain may represent some sort of wish fulfilment: she herself had tried to arrange to visit the country even before the war ended. It is not surprising that she failed, for her left-wing sympathies were well known. For example she helped to promote an anti-Fascist meeting at the Queen's Hall organised by the Association of Writers for Intellectual Liberty. But her anti-Fascist ardour, like her pacifist ardour, was beset with doubts. After that very meeting she wrote to Daniel George, 'I'm glad we had it, though heaven knows what good we think it will do.' And the interminable political discussions in her novel are all of them inconclusive, though at the end of the book there is a hint that she was glimpsing 'an answer' entirely outside politics. It may not be irrelevant that she had just been giving thought to the writings of E. M. Forster. The scene is a bar in St Jean de Luz, and the young

English Marxist finds himself reunited with two of his friends, a Spanish aristocrat and a bourgeois French industrialist. The politics of the three could hardly have been more divergent. But the English boy is no longer angry or bitter. 'Yes', he thought, 'It is people that matter . . . Life was what it was, people what they were. Cruelty was the devil, and most people were, in one way or another, cruel . . . Still, here they sat and talked, three friends together.'

Political controversies dominate *And No Man's Wit*. But throughout the story there runs a refreshing streak of fantasy. The hero's fiancée, a slender, palely beautiful girl, has mermaid blood. In 'Ellen Green', who wilts when out of reach of water, and revives at once on returning to her natural element, Rose was able to express her own passionate love of the sea and bathing. In Ellen's joy, as she escapes from the arid land, can be sensed the joy that Rose, ever since a child, had so often tasted herself.

She . . . waded into the warm, lovely, shimmering stuff that sighed and rustled against her body . . . [and then] swam out to sea . . . "Ellen! Ellen! Come in! We're starting." Ellen did not turn or seem to hear; with her gentle fin-like stroke of the arms, she swam on . . . The slow green swaying world was friendly and cool. Its floor shelved sharply down . . . Absently, without conscious purpose she wriggled out of the stupid, hampering bathing dress, saw it drift wavily, pompously away; she drew a deep breath . . . and knew herself at last part of the ancestral ocean, whose salt tide flows through our veins, beats for ever in our blood. From far off she heard shouts, as of her name being called; vaguely she knew that she was being summoned from her ancient country to that other harsh, hot, dry country full of riddles that she did not understand. She turned her back on it, and gave her white and shimmering body to ocean's arms, drifting gently along wide-eyed. All she saw, she knew; it was like a forgotten dream that returns, or like a home known in childhood and left, and revisited after many years.

Like Ellen, Rose herself found a deep delight in bathing in the nude. In a broadcast talk on the pleasures of bathing which she gave in 1936, at the age of fifty-four, she voiced the following views:

If one is so fortunate as to find a place and a time when one can bathe without a bathing suit, it enormously increases the pleasure of a bathe. The feeling of water, even river water, against one's bare skin is delightful. Besides, you don't have to carry about a wet bathing suit afterwards. I suppose the time is approaching when we shall all bathe unclad as a matter of course; at present it is still only a rare pleasure. All we can do is to make our suits as slight and unhampering as we can.[1]

---

[1] 'In Deep and Shallow Waters', *The Listener*, 20 January 1936.

13

INTO THE ABYSS

ROSE did not go abroad for a summer holiday in 1939; instead she thought she would explore the Lake District, and on 12 June set off north in her Morris. From Keswick she sent a postcard to Daniel George telling him she had driven through the night up the Great North Road: 'Nice empty roads, and a lovely dawn, and a Thermos of tea to keep me going.' There was nothing to suggest that anyone was with her, and we do not know whether Gerald accompanied her on the drive or joined her at Keswick, but it later came to light that they were at the Lakes together. As always they conducted themselves very discreetly, and on this occasion stayed in different hotels. Rose may have insisted on even more care than usual because apparently her identity soon leaked out; when she had been in Keswick a week the local press reported that 'Miss Rose Macaulay, the well known novelist' was staying at the Waverley Hotel. After ten days a second cheery postcard went off to Daniel George, this time 'A Cattle Scene, Derwentwater' with the comment 'I'm glad these cows aren't in literature, so I don't need to collect them. I spend my time trying to hoot them off the moor roads, with little success.' Obviously Rose was enjoying her motoring holiday.

Then two days later, on 26 June, she and Gerald set off for an expedition to the Roman Wall. The drive took them through Penrith and up on to the Fells, and the gradual climb across the moors was by the main road to Alston (A'686), a road with long straights and occasional sudden hairpins. Just before midday they reached Hartside, famous for its breathtaking views, and Rose, as so often, failed to give proper attention to the road ahead. Swerving towards the wrong side of the road as they approached a blind corner they met an oncoming car. With a sickening crash the two cars ended locked together. Miraculously no one was killed. But Gerald had head injuries and Rose suffered badly from shock; as she disentangled herself from the wreckage she kept repeating that it was all her fault. Then she fainted. It was just three and a half years since she had let fly at Lord de Clifford in *The Spectator*.

Various details of the accident are on public record, for three weeks later Rose had to appear in the Penrith Police Court and there was a report in the *Penrith Observer* headed 'VOLUNTEER AMBULANCE DRIVER IN PENRITH COURT: LONDON VISITOR'S CARELESS DRIVING ON HARTSIDE.' The defendant was described as 'a lady motorist, Emily Macaulay', of Luxborough House, Northumberland Street, and Rose must have felt unspeakably relieved that her alias was so effective; by means of this simple device the publicity that would have flared up if the Press had realised that she was 'the well known novelist' was entirely avoided. She pleaded Guilty to the charge of Careless Driving, and evidence was given by the driver of the second car (a Mr Alan Wilson of Gosforth,) a police constable from the village of Melmerby who had accompanied a doctor to the crash, and by Rose herself. She said that she did not know how the accident had happened 'except that her friend (Gerald's name was not mentioned) had called her attention to a signpost and she had looked to the side for a moment.' She added that she must have swerved to the middle of the road without knowing it. The Bench, to her chagrin, decided that her licence must be endorsed; this worried her far more than the fine which was for only two pounds.

There was no hint, in the press report, that anyone involved in the crash had suffered serious after-effects, but this was an omission. Soon after Gerald's head was injured he had a stroke, and for a time it was uncertain whether he would live. Rose, when she was south again, confided her anguished anxiety to Jean, who was just home from South Africa (since 1936 she and Nancy Willetts had been working as missionary nurses), and Jean has never forgotten the broken look on Rose's face when she said 'If he dies, you won't be seeing me for some time.'

Gerald did not die in 1939. He recovered from the stroke. But it is no exaggeration to say that Rose never recovered from the trauma of the accident and its sequel; they haunted her all her life. She kept the secret from almost everyone, but when seventeen years later, in *The Towers of Trebizond*, she described the heroine's distress after the accident when her lover was killed, many felt certain that Rose herself must have been through the same sort of self-accusing agony. One might perhaps imagine that the putting into words of her own experience, even at one remove in a novel, would have helped to free her from her obsession. But when shortly before her death she started on another novel, *Venice Besieged*, she chose as its dramatic opening the repercussions of a road accident in which a man was killed. Like the crash on the Cumberland moors it took place at midsummer.

The accident on Hartside marked the beginning of the most catastrophic period of Rose's life. And at the time when the war started, two months after the accident, she was so immersed in private anxiety that she barely comprehended what was happening. 'This seems a bad dream', she wrote to Daniel George, 'and I still hope to wake before it's too late. I can't really believe it.'

Amidst the uncertainties and tensions of the phoney war Rose did her best to work normally, but she found the final stages of *And No Man's Wit* exceedingly irksome. 'I am dead sick of my novel', she told Daniel George, 'but must push on. I'd so much rather get on to my beasts. But no one would look at them in war-time,

I imagine. And my rent must be paid, alas, and these intimidating taxes. So I put down words, enjoying none of them ... I live in hopes of better days, when ... my Animals can flourish.'

Until France fell she clung to the hope that Britain might be able to pull out of the war, but when the threat of invasion came she underwent a change of heart. According to Jean (who since the outbreak of war had started work again as a district nurse, this time at Romford) Rose's new attitude came into being after a conversation with Sir William Beveridge. 'We really *should* do something more about rubbing it in day and night what an awful England it would be under the Nazis', she now wrote to Jean. 'I hear that it is very common to hear people say it would be as good as it is now, so why not let them come quietly instead of bombing us first? If that spirit grows we are done ... The great thing ... is to embattle everyone's *mind*.' Meanwhile to Daniel George she admitted that her writing did not seem worth while 'when one doesn't know if one will survive to finish anything, or if anyone will survive to print anything ... One fidgets about waiting for the next news.'

Once the Blitz began Rose found herself looking forward to the nights when she was on duty with her ambulance unit, for then, when she was not driving (her accident does not seem to have caused her any loss of nerve) she had a 'nice dug-out' to sit in, with cheerful colleagues for company. At Luxborough House she did not at first even consider spending the night anywhere but in her flat (later she sometimes bedded down under the main staircase). 'I hope you aren't having as noisy a night as we are', she wrote to Jean on 11 September 1940. 'It began just as I got home and has got worse ... I never heard such a deafening and continuous pounding ... The house rocks – but I read to-day that houses can rock a lot without harm ... Oh dear, this is *too* much I must get my wax balls ... I am expecting my ceiling to collapse, and the furniture from the flat above to come through on to me ... How fantastic life has become.'

In another letter to Jean there is an account of a night when she was on duty. 'I went out with an ambulance from 10 till 4 a.m. . . . Bombing was v. bad all round that night; I attended an incident in Camden Town – two fallen houses, a great pile of ruins, with all the inhabitants buried deep. The demolition men worked and hacked away very skilfully and patiently, and we all encouraged the people inside, telling them they would be out in a short time, but of course they weren't. There was a mother and a crying baby, who were rescued at 10.0 next morning after I had gone. I drove to hospital another mother, who had left two small children under the ruins. I told her they would be out very soon – but they never were, they were killed. The demolition men are splendid – we passed milk down to the baby, and water for the others, and the men kept saying to them "It'll be all right, dear. Don't you worry." They are very nice and matey. I like their way of calling every one (including the ambulance women) "mate". So polite, too. One of them was using some language about the bombs that whistled round, when his companion saw me just behind and said "Look out, lady here", and he said "Sorry, Miss, excuse my language." I assured him I felt the same way myself. They are, of course, so used to the job (every night) that they can throw it off when they are relieved, and think about other things . . . I am still an amateur at it and it rather gets one down.'

Each week that autumn Rose went to Romford for Jean's day off, groping her way home in the blackout through the 'bombs and guns and flashes'. One night, on her return, she found Luxborough House deserted except for a policeman guarding the door. A time-bomb had fallen nearby and everyone had been advised to move out. But Rose evidently did not regard such advice as applying to herself, and from her flat she wrote to Jean, 'I am here alone for the night, hoping that if the bomb goes off it won't break my windows, which I have opened top and bottom. I have been sitting on the stairs by the street door for a time, talking to the policeman and giving him a drink of sherry . . . He says he is "scared blue" very often, and so are all the police, firemen, wardens etc.' Next day she added a P.S.: 'Luxborough still stands. But London is more and more a devastated area . . . bicycling to Soho to lunch, diverted at every street by ruins, craters, and ropes, took an incredible time.'

She was still managing to see something of her friends, and meetings with Harold Nicolson, Middleton Murry, and the Gollanczs are mentioned in her letters. She also saw Gilbert Murray occasionally when he was in London. Ever since childhood she had known and admired 'Professor Murray' as a distinguished friend of her father's (he was fifteen years her senior) but now in wartime they began to make friends as fellow writers and soon discovered many tastes in common, ranging from brains trusts and detective stories to broadcasts of Greek plays and chats on the political situation.

Another friend with whom Rose kept in touch was Virginia Woolf, though they were not able to meet after the Woolfs' house in Mecklenburgh Square had been bombed. In October 1940, five months before Virginia's death, Rose wrote to her:

How I wish I could see you! It's one of the sad things about this war, seeing people has become so much more difficult, at the same time more important. I like it so much when I do see you . . . I would like to talk about . . . Coleridge . . . some time, as I have long had in mind a novel about a girl who would be his descendant (great great grandchild, the fruit of mild and rural sin) and would take after him. I suppose she would be a very odd girl, wouldn't she – opium, metaphysics, flow of talk, cadging on friends, even poetry, but it needn't be as good as his. I don't know if I shall ever write her – or, indeed, if one will ever write anything. Even my Animals languish, as there is so little time, and one feels (a) sleepy (b) mentally disintegrated. I expect this war is thoroughly demoralizing. We shall emerge (so far as we do emerge) scattered in wits, many of us troglodytes, others all agog for new excitements each day. The interest each day is discovering which was 'the famous street', 'the historic square', 'the fashionable church', etc. I'm sorry Mecklenburgh was among these. Round me there are rather a lot of smashes. I have always said I will *not* be buried alive but cremated instead, and shall feel it unjust if these orders are disregarded by God . . . I like my ambulance colleagues, male and female. You would too, I think. They teach me to knit, and are not unduly cast down by what they have to see and to do. I always hope that victims beneath the ruins are a little stupefied by their odd predicament, and don't feel their position quite so acutely as one might suppose, though they do make agonizing conversation often.

Rose's idea for a novel about a descendant of Coleridge never came to anything, though she told Daniel George that she wanted to give it priority: 'I shall, I think, do the novel first, then turn back to the "Animals", on the chance that the times may by then be propitious for them. But I foresee that they may be my life-companion, and perhaps it is as well, as I like them as company very much: they may solace my declining years. But again, who knows? Any time . . . things may crack, and one lives from day to day.' From day to day . . . and from night to night. Twice before the end of October, once in daylight and once in a night raid, Luxborough House was very nearly hit: on both occasions Rose was out of her flat. 'I returned from a walk this afternoon to find that for the second time . . . a bomb had fallen in the . . . garden under our windows', she wrote to Daniel George on 25 October, 'and had blown out all the cardboard with which the windows had been replaced last Friday, smashed some more china, brought down some more ceiling, and generally played the hooligan in my flat. It is annoying, but of course we are lucky, having been attacked twice, not to have got a direct hit and been reduced to a heap of rubble. The first time I was at my ambulance station, and just as well, as the bed I should have been in was strewn and cut with glass from my window.'

During the early months of 1941, through the latter part of the Blitz, Rose was mostly out of London. She was having to be at Liss for a distressing reason; it had been found that Margaret, who was now sixty, was suffering from cancer – an unexpected shock. She died mercifully soon on 1 March, and then for Rose there was the depressing job of sorting and disposing of her things. The circumstances were doubly sad, for not only had a beloved sister been lost but a family home was being broken up.

Two months elapsed before Rose had completed her sorting. Most of the furniture and many of the books were to be sold, but certain things were to go to members of the family. She was still at Liss at the beginning of May when the removers came to collect the batches for herself and Jean. And it so happened that the van set off for Luxborough House and Romford just after London had suffered its last raid of the Blitz, the heavy attack on the night of 10 May, when the House of Commons, Westminster Hall, and the British Museum were hit. Eventually the van reached Romford, and Jean can still remember the moment when she learnt the shattering news that Rose's flat had been destroyed in the big raid. When the men had tried to make their delivery to Luxborough House they had found nothing but ruins and rubble.

'Forgive this dislocated scrawl written in train to Romford to spend night with my sister', Rose scribbled on an odd scrap of paper to Daniel George on the evening of 14 May. 'I came up last night from Liss to find Lux: House no more – bombed and burned out of existence, and *nothing* saved. I am bookless, homeless, sans everything but my eyes to weep with. *All* my (and your) notes on animals gone – I shall never write that book now. I don't expect you kept any notes of what you copied for me . . . I shall take a room somewhere, till I can look round . . . I had a borrowed typewriter with me at Liss; little else, but the clothes I am wearing. What does one do? I have no O[xford] D[ictionary]. No Purchas. No nothing ... It would have been less trouble to have been bombed myself.'

Not only in the first stunned bewilderment, but later too, the loss of her books caused Rose extreme anguish. Another flat could be found; her furniture could be replaced – in fact readily so, for the sale of Margaret's belongings could be cancelled. But her books ... To Rose her books were her intimate, beloved friends, the companions of her daily life. 'The less I brood over my lost darlings', she wrote in her next letter to Daniel George, 'the better for my sanity.' To Gilbert Murray, in reply to a letter of sympathy, she used more measured terms but there was no disguising her grief. 'I do indeed feel destitute and bereaved without my books – they were the heritage of 4 generations of book-lovers, besides my own collection. Nothing can replace them. But I have begun to try round for some of them at the second-hand booksellers. And Logan Pearsall Smith, whom I saw yesterday, has given me some of his, and returned me some I had lent him ... I don't know what one does ... I have little heart for anything.'

For about a month Rose was homeless, and she used a bed-sitting room in Manchester Street as a base. Jean offered to have her at Romford and various friends begged her to come and stay, but she preferred to be alone and excused herself by explaining that she had to be near her ruin. 'First I was scrambling up my ruin after salvage', she told Daniel George, '[and] I got my May and June marmalade ration, and a few bits of glass and china – of all things – which had been marvellously guarded in my kitchen dresser – all else burnt to ashes.' Her cousin Jean Smith was giving her what help she could, lending her clothes, and sharing in the preparations for moving into a new flat. Everyone was wonderfully kind. But nothing could ease the pain of having lost her books.

Many of her publisher friends, when they heard of her loss, hastened to offer replacements, and S. C. Roberts volunteered to look out for any books she specially wanted. 'I am getting on slowly with re-booking', she wrote to him. '[But] I hesitate to get valuable books yet, for I foresee a rather violent few months ahead and I couldn't bear this loss twice.' The books she missed most of all were the volumes of her Oxford Dictionary, and her joy was unbounded when the Gollanczs presented her with a new set. 'What can I say, and wherewith can I thank you?...My darling Dictionary again, in the same vestage and habit as I have always known . . . I think it is the most generous act of friendship I ever knew . . . I begin to feel I can live again. The O.D. was my Bible, my staff, my entertainer, my help in work and my recreation in leisure – nothing else serves. Bless you a thousand hundred times for angels!... My new flat already looks lovely in my mind's eye, its shelves abloom with those dark red vols. Oh God, if H. bombs it now! I thought I didn't care – but now I do. What hostages to fortune one gives.'

The new flat that Rose found was in Hinde Street off Manchester Square, and she moved to 20 Hinde House in the second week of June 1941. Slightly smaller than her previous flat it suited her well, and was her home for the rest of her life. Once she had settled in, her mind turned to writing again, but she was in no mood to embark on a novel. 'I'm not much good at ordinary novels just now, I think', she confessed to Daniel George. 'Am I tired of private lives? I mustn't get like that or it will be the end of me as a novelist. I know they are what matter, of course, but I can't be interested at the moment, only in mass movements – how disgusting!' This last remark referred to a book, or rather a longish essay, *Life Among the English*, that she was writing for a Collins series *Britain in Pictures*. She quite enjoyed working on it at first, but before she had finished it her health gave way; in November she developed a gastric ulcer. This meant complete rest and a milk diet, first in King's College Hospital and then with Jean at Romford.

By the New Year she was feeling well enough to compose some lighthearted doggerel verses in honour of a new goddaughter, Mary Anne O'Donovan, Gerald's first grandchild. But she was still very weak, and decided to resign from the Ambulance Service. Her writing was almost at a standstill. Just at this time, however, she did produce one piece of writing of outstanding quality, a moving short story called 'Miss Anstruther's Letters'. She wrote it because Storm Jameson had persuaded her to contribute to a collection of topical writing, *London Calling*, that she was editing for publication in America. 'Miss Anstruther's Letters', one of the few short stories Rose ever wrote, was concerned (so she mentioned casually to Daniel George) with a bombed flat. 'Unoriginal', she added, 'but veracious (mainly).'

By this time Rose and Daniel George were in the habit of lunching together quite often, but in June she wrote to say that she found it difficult to suggest a day for their next meeting, because she was having to be out of London several times each week – this was over and above her trips to Romford. These additional expeditions were to Albury in Surrey where Gerald and his wife were now living, and the reason why she was going there so often was that Gerald was dying of cancer. He died on 26 July 1942.[1] Two weeks later *The Times* published in their obituary columns a short tribute to him 'from a friend'; it had been written by Rose, mostly in a formal style.

Gerald O'Donovan, who died at Albury, Surrey, on July 26, was best known as a writer by his first novel, *Father Ralph*, which was, like his later novels, a careful, able, documentary, and in parts brilliant presentment of Irish life, the life he knew and grew up in. He was a man of wide and versatile interests; he was successively sub-warden of Toynbee Hall, publisher, and head of the Italian Section of Crewe House during the

[1] His widow survived him for over fifteen years; she died on 6 April 1968.

last war. From 1938 on, until his health failed, he threw himself into the assistance of Czech refugees; his sympathetic understanding of their problems was a characteristic example of the generous help he always gave to those in need. As a friend he never failed; his wise judgment and unstinting interest were always on tap behind his reserve and behind the sometimes sardonic wit that was his Irish heritage.

And then came a final sentence, a spontaneous postscript in an utterly different tone, a remark straight from the heart: 'To know him was to love him.'

14

'MISS ANSTRUTHER'S LETTERS'

As a finale to this tragic chapter of Rose's life it is fitting to include here a testimony of her love for Gerald O'Donovan, which she wrote under the conventional veil of fiction. 'Miss Anstruther's Letters' was written before Gerald's death, but while he was dying. It appeared in America in 1942 in *London Calling* but has not previously been published in Britain.

Miss Anstruther's Letters

Miss Anstruther, whose life had been cut in two on the night of May 10th, 1941, so that she now felt herself a ghost, without attachments or habitation, neither of which she any longer desired, sat alone in the bed-sitting-room she had taken, a small room, littered with the grimy, broken and useless objects which she had salvaged from the burnt-out ruin round the corner. It was one of the many burnt-out ruins of that wild night when high explosives and incendiaries had rained on London and the water had run short: it was now a gaunt and roofless tomb, a pile of ashes and rubble and burnt, smashed beams. Where the floors of twelve flats had been there was empty space. Miss Anstruther had for the first few days climbed up to what had been her flat, on what had been the third floor, swarming up pendent fragments of beams and broken girders, searching and scrabbling among

ashes and rubble, but not finding what she sought, only here a
pot, there a pan, sheltered from destruction by an overhanging
slant of ceiling. Her marmalade for May had been there, and a
little sugar and tea; the demolition men got the sugar and tea, but
did not care for marmalade, so Miss Anstruther got that. She did
not know what else went into those bulging dungaree pockets,
and did not really care, for she knew it would not be the thing
she sought, for which even demolition men would have no use;
the flames, which take anything, useless or not, had taken these,
taken them and destroyed them like a ravaging mouse or an idiot
child.

After a few days the police had stopped Miss Anstruther from
climbing up to her flat any more, since the building was scheduled
as dangerous. She did not much mind; she knew by then that
what she looked for was gone for good. It was not among the
massed debris on the basement floor, where piles of burnt,
soaked and blackened fragments had fallen through four floors to
lie in indistinguishable anonymity together. The tenant of the
basement flat spent her days there, sorting and burrowing among
the chaotic mass that had invaded her home from the dwellings
of her co-tenants above. There were masses of paper, charred and
black and damp, which had been books. Sometimes the basement
tenant would call out to Miss Anstruther, 'Here's a book. That'll
be yours, Miss Anstruther'; for it was believed in Mortimer House
that most of the books contained in it were Miss Anstruther's,
Miss Anstruther being something of a bookworm. But none of
the books were any use now, merely drifts of burnt pages. Most
of the pages were loose and scattered about the rubbish-heaps;
Miss Anstruther picked up one here and there and made out some
words. 'Yes', she would agree. 'Yes, that was one of mine.' The
basement tenant, digging bravely away for her motoring
trophies, said 'Is it one you wrote?' 'I don't think so', said Miss
Anstruther. 'I don't think I can have . . .' She did not really know
what she might not have written, in that burnt-out past when she

had sat and written this and that on the third floor, looking out on green gardens; but she did not think it could have been this, which was a page from Urquhart's translation of Rabelais. 'Have you lost *all* your own?' the basement tenant asked, thinking about her motoring cups, and how she must get at them before the demolition men did, for they were silver. 'Everything', Miss Anstruther answered. 'Everything. They don't matter.' 'I hope you had no precious manuscripts', said the kind tenant. 'Books you were writing, and that.' 'Yes', said Miss Anstruther, digging about among the rubble heaps. 'Oh yes. They're gone. They don't matter . . .'

She went on digging till twilight came. She was grimed from head to foot; her only clothes were ruined; she stood knee-deep in drifts of burnt rubbish that had been carpets, beds, curtains, furniture, pictures, and books; the smoke that smouldered up from them made her cry and cough. What she looked for was not there; it was ashes, it was no more. She had not rescued it while she could, she had forgotten it, and now it was ashes. All but one torn, burnt corner of notepaper, which she picked up out of a battered saucepan belonging to the basement tenant. It was niggled over with close small writing, the only words left of the thousands of words in that hand that she looked for. She put it in her note-case and went on looking till dark; then she went back to her bed-sitting-room, which she filled each night with dirt and sorrow and a few blackened cups.

She knew at last that it was no use to look any more, so she went to bed and lay open-eyed through the short summer nights. She hoped each night that there would be another raid, which should save her the trouble of going on living. But it seemed that the Luftwaffe had, for the moment, done; each morning came, the day broke, and like a revenant, Miss Anstruther still haunted her ruins, where now the demolition men were at work, digging and sorting and pocketing as they worked.

'I watch them close', said a policeman standing by. 'I always hope I'll catch them at it. But they sneak into dark corners and stuff their pockets before you can look round.'

'They didn't ought', said the widow of the publican who had kept the little smashed pub on the corner, 'they didn't ought to let them have those big pockets, it's not right. Poor people like us, who've lost all we had, to have what's left taken off us by *them* . . . it's not right.'

The policeman agreed that it was not right, but they were that crafty, he couldn't catch them at it.

Each night, as Miss Anstruther lay awake in her strange, littered, unhomely room, she lived again the blazing night that had cut her life in two. It had begun like other nights, with the wailing siren followed by the crashing guns, the rushing hiss of incendiaries over London, and the whining, howling, pitching of bombs out of the sky on to the fire-lit city. A wild, blazing hell of a night. Miss Anstruther, whom bombs made restless, had gone down once or twice to the street door to look at the glowing furnace of London and exchange comments with the caretaker on the ground floor and with the two basement tenants, then she had sat on the stairs, listening to the demon noise. Crashes shook Mortimer House, which was tall and slim and Edwardian, and swayed like a reed in the wind to near bombing. Miss Anstruther understood that this was a good sign, a sign that Mortimer House, unlike the characters ascribed to clients by fortune-tellers, would bend but not break. So she was quite surprised and shocked when, after a series of three close-at-hand screams and crashes, the fourth exploded, a giant earthquake, against Mortimer House, and sent its whole front crashing down. Miss Anstruther, dazed and bruised from the hurtle of bricks and plaster flung at her head, and choked with dust, hurried down the stairs, which were still there. The wall on the street was a pile of smoking, rumbling rubble, the Gothic respectability of Mortimer House one with Nineveh and Tyre and with the little public [*sic*] across the street. The ground-floor flats, the hall and the street outside, were scrambled and beaten into a common devastation of smashed masonry and dust. The little caretaker was tugging at his large wife, who was struck unconscious and jammed to the knees in bricks. The basement tenant, who had rushed up with her stirrup pump, began to tug too, so did Miss Anstruther. Policemen pushed in through the mess, rescue men and a warden followed, all was in train for rescue, as Miss Anstruther had so often seen it in her ambulance-driving.

'What about the flats above?' they called. 'Any one in them?'

Only two of the flats above had been occupied, Miss Anstruther's at the back. Mrs Cavendish's at the front. The rescuers rushed upstairs to investigate the fate of Mrs Cavendish.

'Why the devil', enquired the police, 'wasn't every one downstairs?' But the caretaker's wife, who had been downstairs, was unconscious and jammed, while Miss Anstruther, who had been upstairs, was neither.

They hauled out the caretaker's wife, and carried her to a waiting ambulance.

'Everyone out of the building!' shouted the police. 'Everyone out!'

Miss Anstruther asked why.

The police said there were to be no bloody whys, everyone out, the bloody gas pipe's burst and they're throwing down fire, the whole thing may go up in a bonfire before you can turn round.

A bonfire! Miss Anstruther thought, if that's so I must go up and save some things. She rushed up the stairs, while the rescue men were in Mrs Cavendish's flat. Inside her own blasted and twisted door, her flat lay waiting for death. God, muttered Miss Anstruther, what shall I save? She caught up a suitcase, and furiously piled books into it – Herodotus, *Mathematical Magick*, some of the twenty volumes of *Purchas his Pilgrimes*, the eight little volumes of Walpole's letters, *Trivia, Curiosities of Literature*, the six volumes of Boswell, then, as the suitcase would not shut, she turned out Boswell and substituted a china cow, a tiny walnut shell with tiny Mexicans behind glass, a box with a mechanical bird that jumped out and sang, and a fountain pen. No use bothering with the big books or the pictures. Slinging the suitcase across her back, she caught up her portable wireless set and her typewriter, loped down stairs, placed her salvage on the piled wreckage at what had been the street door, and started up the stairs again. As she reached the first floor, there was a burst and a hissing, a huge *pst-pst*, and a rush of flame leaped over Mortimer House as the burst gas caught and sprang to heaven, another fiery rose bursting into bloom to join that pandemonic red garden of night. Two rescue men, carrying Mrs Cavendish downstairs, met Miss Anstruther and pushed her back.

'Clear out. Can't get up there again, it'll go up any minute.'

It was at this moment that Miss Anstruther remembered the thing she wanted most, the thing she had forgotten while she gathered up things she wanted less.

She cried, 'I must go up again. I must get something out. There's time.'

'Not a bloody second', one of them shouted at her, and pushed her back.

She fought him. 'Let me go, oh let me go. I tell you I'm going up once more.'

On the landing above, a wall of flame leaped crackling to the ceiling.

'Go up be damned. Want to go through that?'

They pulled her down with them to the ground floor. She ran out into the street, shouting for a ladder. Oh God, where are the fire engines? A hundred fires, the water given out in some places, engines helpless. Everywhere buildings burning, museums, churches, hospitals, great shops, houses, blocks of flats, north, south, east, west and centre. Such a raid never was. Miss Anstruther heeded none of it: with hell blazing and crashing round her, all she thought was, I must get my letters. Oh, dear God, my letters. She pushed again into the inferno, but again she was dragged back. 'No one to go in there,' said the police, for all human life was by now extricated. No one to go in, and Miss Anstruther's flat left to be consumed in the spreading storm of fire, which was to leave no wrack behind. Everything was doomed – furniture, books, pictures, china, clothes, manuscripts, silver, everything: all she thought of was the desk crammed with letters that should have been the first thing she saved. What had she saved instead? Her wireless, her typewriter, a suitcase full of books; looking round, she saw that all three had gone from where she had put them down. Perhaps they were in the safe keeping of the police, more likely in the wholly unsafe keeping of some rescue-squad man or private looter. Miss Anstruther cared little. She sat down on the wreckage of the road, sick and shaking, wholly bereft.

The bombers departed, their job well done. Dawn came, dim and ashy, in a pall of smoke. The little burial garden was like a garden in a Vesuvian village, grey in its ash coat. The air choked with fine drifts of cinders, Mortimer House still burned, for no one had put it out. A grimy warden with a note-book asked Miss Anstruther, have you anywhere to go?

'No', she said, 'I shall stay here.'

'Better go to a rest centre', said the warden, wearily doing his job, not caring where any one went, wondering what had happened in North Ealing, where he lived.

Miss Anstruther stayed, watching the red ruin smouldering low. Some time, she thought, it will be cool enough to go into.

There followed the haunted, desperate days of search which found nothing. Since silver and furniture had been wholly consumed, what hope for letters? There was no charred sliver of the old locked rosewood desk which had held them. The burning words were burnt, the lines, running small and close and neat down the page, difficult to decipher, with the o's and a's never closed at the top, had run into a flaming void and would never be deciphered more. Miss Anstruther tried to recall them, as she sat in the alien room; shutting her eyes, she tried to see again the phrases that, once you had made them out, lit the page like stars. There had been many hundreds of letters, spread over twenty-two years. Last year their writer had died; the letters were all that Miss Anstruther had left of him; she had not yet re-read them; she had been waiting till she could do so without the devastation of unendurable weeping. They had lain there, a solace waiting for her when she could take it. Had she taken it, she could have recalled them better now. As it was, her memory held disjointed phrases, could not piece them together. Light of my eyes. You are the sun and the moon and the stars to me. When I think of you life becomes music, poetry, beauty, and I am more than myself. It is what lovers have found in all the ages, and no one has ever found before. The sun flickering through the beeches on your hair. And so on. As each phrase came back to her, it jabbed at her heart like a twisting bayonet. He would run over a list of places they had seen together, in the secret stolen travels of twenty years. The balcony where they dined at the Foix inn, leaning over the green river, eating trout just caught in it. The little wild strawberries at Andorra la Vieja, the mountain pass that ran down to it from Ax, the winding road down into Seo d'Urgel and Spain. Lerida, Zaragoza, little mountain towns in the Pyrenees, Jaca, Saint Jean Pied-du-Port, the little harbour at Collioure, with its painted boats, morning coffee out of red cups at Villefranche, tramping about France in a hot July; truffles in the *place* at Perigueux, the stream that rushed steeply down the village street at Florac, the frogs croaking in the hills about it, the gorges of the Tarn, Rodez with its spacious *place* and plane trees, the little walled town of Cordes with the inn courtyard a jumble of sculptures, altar-pieces from churches, and ornaments from chateaux; Lisieux, with ancient crazy-floored inn, huge four-poster, and preposterous little saint (before the grandiose white temple in her honour had arisen on the hill outside the town), villages in the Haute-Savoie, jumbled among mountain rocks over brawling streams, the motor bus over the Alps down into Susa and Italy. Walking over the Amberley downs, along the Dorset coast from Corfe to Lyme on two hot May days, with a night at Chideock between, sauntering in Buckinghamshire beech-woods, boating off Bucklers Hard, climbing Dunkery Beacon to Porlock, driving on a June afternoon over Kirkdale pass . . . Baedeker starred places because we ought to see them, he wrote, I star them because we saw them together, and those stars light them up for ever . . . Of this kind had been many of the letters that had been for the last year all Miss Anstruther had left, except memory, of two-and-twenty years. There had been other letters about books, books he was reading, books she was writing; others about plans, politics, health, the weather, himself, herself, anything. I could have saved them, she kept thinking; I had the chance; but I saved a typewriter and a wireless set and some books and a walnut shell and a china cow, and even they are gone. So she would cry and cry, till tears blunted at last for the time the sharp edge of grief, leaving only a dull lassitude, an end of being. Sometimes she would take out and look at the charred corner of paper which was now all she had of her lover; all that was legible of it was a line and a half of close small writing, the o's and the a's open at the top. It had been written twenty-one years ago, and it said, 'leave it at that. I know now that you don't care twopence; if you did you would' . . . The words, each time she looked at them, seemed to darken and obliterate a little more of the twenty years that had followed them, the years of the letters and the starred places and all they had had together. You don't care twopence, he seemed to say still; if you had cared twopence, you would have saved my letters, not your wireless and your typewriter and your china cow, least of all those little walnut Mexicans, which you know I never liked. Leave it at that.

Oh, if instead of these words she had found light of my eyes, or I think of the balcony at Foix, she thought she could have gone on living. As it is, thought Miss Anstruther, as it is I can't. Oh my darling, I did care twopence, I did.

Later, she took another flat. Life assembled itself about her again; kind friends gave her books; she bought another type-writer, another wireless set, and ruined herself with getting necessary furniture, for which she would get no financial help until after the war. She noticed little of all this that she did, and saw no real reason for doing any of it. She was alone with a past devoured by fire and a charred scrap of paper which said you don't care twopence, and then a blank, a great interruption, an end. She had failed in caring once, twenty years ago, and failed again now, and the twenty years between were a drift of grey ashes that once were fire, and she a drifting ghost too. She had to leave it at that.

PART III

Homecoming
1943 – 1958

15

IBERIA

'A WESTERN OASIS in the frightening desert': this was how Rose described Portugal in 1943, just after she had spent two blissful months there. Her pretext for escaping from the drabness of war was research for a new book, a non-fiction book on an unusual aspect of Anglo-Portuguese relations; it was to be an account of the many English who through the centuries had visited Portugal, from the Crusaders to the Victorians. 'I couldn't have done a novel possibly', she later wrote, looking back to the time after Gerald's death. 'I always talked over my novels with my companion, who stimulated my invention; when he died my mind seemed to go blank and dead . . . I was very unhappy just then, and had to deaden it with work.'[1] So she had deliberately chosen a subject that would mean an immense amount of research.

In March she set off for Lisbon. 'I hope there will still be an England on my return', she wrote to Daniel George before she left. She went in one of the small civil planes with boarded-up windows that plied regularly between Britain and neutral Portugal, and there were no mishaps en route, though things might well have been otherwise. It was only a few weeks later that Leslie Howard, whose lecture tour for the British Council overlapped with Rose's visit, met his death returning to London when the aircraft in which he was a passenger was shot down by an enemy plane.

In Lisbon, then Europe's main port of transit to the outside world, Rose took time off from her work in various libraries to

[1] *Letters to a Friend*, p. 116.

share in the social life, and she made several lasting friendships, notably with Luis Marques and his wife Susan (daughter of Mrs Belloc Lowndes) two leading figures in Anglo-Portuguese society, and David Ley, a Lecturer at the British Institute. She also went on several expeditions and the country enchanted her: 'Everything is so beautiful and graceful and attractively coloured – the little towns, the steep streets, the tiny donkeys between great panniers of oranges, the women at the fountains with their great Moorish red pots, the oxen about the streets of Oporto with their carved yokes, the glimpses of the Tagus, blue and green and grey.'[1]

Back again in wartime London she immersed herself in her book, *They Went to Portugal*, and spent much time working in the British Museum Reading Room and the Public Records Office. Indeed her 'Portugal book' was her main occupation for the rest of the war, and she persevered with it in spite of recurrent gastric trouble, and also in spite of Hitler. When the flying bombs began, in the summer of 1944, she declined a pressing invitation from Gilbert Murray to come to Oxford: 'It is extremely nice to be invited to Yatscombe, and I should love to come . . . if I weren't so tied up in Portugal. But I must keep on at it; and this means Records Office, and about twenty books round me for each separate bit I tackle. If I left it, even for a few days, I should get hazy about what I was doing and lose my way . . . I really don't particularly . . . mind the doodlebugs . . . I find I can sleep quite well in between them, though the noisier bangs, and even the doodling, and still more the sirens (against which, like Ulysses, I cere my ears, with less success than he) do wake one up a good deal. When they are just overhead, I will them to go on and not stop, and put my head under my pillow (if it's night) in case they disobey me. So far they haven't.'

By the beginning of 1945 Rose had written nearly a quarter of a million words on English visitors to Portugal: queens, princes,

[1] R.M. to Gilbert Murray, October 1943.

pirates, monks, poets, merchants, nuns, diplomats, dilettantes, sightseers. 'Her book . . . is big enough for 2 Vols', Will commented to Jean from Canada. 'This no doubt accounts for the time it is taking though I didn't know there were that many English in Portugal.'[1] Rose submitted her typescript to Collins who much to her disappointment refused it. But it was accepted by Jonathan Cape, largely thanks to Daniel George who was now one of their readers. At least they accepted half of it; even this was going to add up to more than four hundred pages.

When *They Went to Portugal* was published, in 1946, Rose sent a copy to Gilbert Murray with apologies for its length. But he assured her that it was not a bit too long. 'What a queer and delightful book you have made out of what seems an impossible subject! . . . I suppose it is mostly your style that makes the charm of it . . . but the actual stories of most of the people are interesting in themselves . . . I wonder if the people who went to Portugal were funnier than those who did not, or whether you could write just as amusingly about the first fifty people who went past the Marble Arch on Saturday.' 'As to the funniness of visitors to Portugal', Rose replied, 'I expect, as you suggest, that most people are pretty funny in parts. But I do feel that British tourists abroad have been rather comic on the whole – so fatuously priggish often, so stuck-up about the "dirt and superstition" they detect abroad. I am sure our manners have improved, however, since the days of Southey, Byron, Borrow, and all the 18th century travellers. We have learned more understanding and tolerance of foreigners, even if we have also learnt to blow them to bits.'

For many years Rose had been longing to explore Spain; in the past she had seen little more of it than Majorca and parts of the Pyrenees and the Basque coast. Even at the time when her

---

[1] Throughout the war Will kept in touch with his sisters by letter. At this time he was suffering from serious heart trouble, and he died after a heart attack on 14 November 1945.

thoughts were concentrated on Portugal the idea of Spain was in her mind. 'I think when the war is over I shall try and visit Spain', she wrote to David Ley in 1943. 'It would be fun. And one of the only countries left to visit; the others will mostly be smashed to bits. I shall get the ancient Morris that is mouldering in a garage, and fling it across the Channel.'

Once the war was over, Spain beckoned with increasing urgency and Rose cast around for a means of financing a trip. Writing to David Ley, who was by now with the British Council in Madrid, she mentioned that Raymond Mortimer had just left for Rome and Athens to lecture on The Novel and added, 'I think I must try to arrange to do some equally useless performance in Madrid! Not lecturing, for that I should hate. I wish I played some musical instrument, sang, danced, or acted. Or why not read poetry aloud, as do all the foreign visitors here?' Her chance came in the spring of 1947. Hamish Hamilton, who was launching a new series of travel books, invited her to undertake one of the first of them. Her subject was to be the eastern and southern seaboards of the Iberian peninsula, which were then 'less well known'. It is a sad irony that Fabled Shore, the delightful travel-diary that Rose wrote for this series, undoubtedly contributed towards the earliest 'development' of the Costa Brava. What would Rose exclaim if she could see her 'fabled shore' today!

Shortly before she left on her Spanish expedition she wrote in high spirits to Gilbert Murray to describe her programme. 'Your scheme of travel is breath-taking', he replied. 'What it is to have youth and courage[1] . . . I am quite frightened of even going to Paris and making a speech. I believe the really restful thing to do is to write a book in ten volumes or so, like Arnold [Toynbee]. People who write lots of short things, like you and me, have constantly to make the effort of starting afresh. You have publishers to spur and bribe you, which makes it easier no doubt.'

This was Rose's first motoring trip abroad since Gerald's death

[1] He was 81, she 66.

Will, Eleanor, Margaret, Jean & Rose (*l. to r.*)

Rose in America (1929)

Jean Macaulay

and she would have preferred not to be alone. But David Ley, whom she invited to join her, was not free to come. Once in Spain however she was far too thrilled to be lonely. 'I am seeing beautiful things', she wrote to Jean from Barcelona. '[Though] a sad number of old churches blown up in the Civil War by the Reds . . . The drive along the zig-zag mountain road above the sea yesterday, between San Felíu de Guixols and Tossa, was magnificent – rather like the steepest and windingest parts of the road above the Italian coast but higher and steeper and more zig-zag. Fortunately there are very few cars, and I only met, in that 30 miles, one mule-cart and two civil guards who inspected my papers . . . Some of the roads atrocious, and very hard on my tyres, which are causing me some anxiety.'

A feature of motoring in Spain in the 1940s which Rose found embarrassing was the vociferousness of the Spanish at the sight of a woman driver. 'All over Spain', she wrote in *Fabled Shore*, 'except in the more sophisticated cities, my driving by was greeted with the same cry – a long, shrill cat-call, reminiscent of a pig having its throat cut, usually wordless, but sometimes accompanied by "*Olé! Olé! una Señora que conduce!*".' 'Women don't drive cars in Spain', she explained to Gilbert Murray, 'and the sight of one doing so amazes and rather shocks them . . . an irritating attitude, no doubt unchanged since Moorish days. In fact, a woman travelling about alone at all astonishes them. As a rather intelligent man said to me "We Spanish don't live in this century at all, but several centuries back" – and it is quite true. When I next meet Sr. Madariaga I shall ask him about this and why he thinks it is. It is interesting. But I should hate to be a woman in Spain. Even the little girls have a poor time, while their brothers are let to play in the streets and ride donkeys about. A Spanish woman told me this was "*una vieja costumbre español*", and one can't get beyond that in analysing it. But the peasant women are splendid, and do all kinds of work in the fields, and drive donkey carts to market by themselves; I felt inclined to say sometimes, "If your women drive donkeys, why shouldn't I drive a car?".'

To Rose, as she pressed on along the coast in the sweltering heat, some of the ways of the Spanish seemed unnecessarily lethargic, and their habit of leaving churches locked often irritated her. 'It seems they have siestas most of the day', she complained to David Ley. 'I prefer the careless, free and easy Anglican way of leaving them open and taking a chance. I also prefer the Anglican way of going into Church in any clothes one has on, without those intimidating warnings on the door to ladies who go in without stockings or with skirts too short. But how grand the churches are outside! One magnificent Catalan Romanesque or Gothic after another, standing high above some little tiled town. It is very wonderful to be back in the Middle Ages, with so little changed; is it because the Spanish lacked money to destroy and rebuild, or because they have less progressive energy? Both, probably. The result is astounding. Tarragona takes one's breath away: except [for] the Ampurias ruins, it is the best thing I have seen. Sagunto is fine (at least the Roman there is) but the Saguntonese [children] are rather much. They never see foreigners, so chase them about with shrieks of derision.'

The rudeness of the young Spaniards was an ordeal that Rose had to undergo time and again. She seems to have realised that their ridicule was not aimed especially at herself (in *Fabled Shore* she told of an unfortunate Frenchwoman being subjected to the same treatment). But her tone when she told David Ley about the 'hoots of rather hostile mirth' suggests that she could not help feeling wounded. 'It is a little like a swarm of midges buzzing round me . . . A woman said to me that the children to-day were very ill-educated and bad. They certainly seem lacking in manners . . . The British Consulate in Barcelona said they are really very conventional people at heart, and anything they aren't used to annoys as well as amuses them . . . Odd that they should be so interested . . . But *how* kind they are if you ask them the way or anything.'

After completing her 'professional' journey at Cape St Vincent Rose went on to Lisbon and spent a happy day at Estoril with the Marqueses. But driving in the capital was a terrifying experience. 'I never know what the police mean by their signals', she wrote to David Ley, 'and everyone hoots all the time, and trucks and carts crash by me hitting my wings in the most ruthless and reckless way.' A dramatic adventure occurred one evening when she was to dine at the British Embassy. 'I caused great excitement . . . when, on turning on my engine, the petrol pipe fused and a fire blazed up under the bonnet. In a moment I seemed surrounded by hundreds of Lisbonians and the whole police force, all shouting at the top of their voices and trying to drag things out of the car, till I stopped this. We soon put out the fire with earth and dust, but meanwhile some excited policeman had sent for the fire brigade, who arrived all equipped with helmets and hose, and were rather cross at finding no fire. I said to the hall porter at the [Hotel] Lis *"Quelle Agitation!"* to which he replied that he supposed in London such an event would be taken with greater calm. I said it would, rather.'

From Lisbon Rose set off north-eastwards across the mountains; she had not originally meant to visit Madrid, but found that she had to go there to obtain photographs for her book. Then she returned once more to the Mediterranean coast, to Valencia, a city she found particularly attractive, at least in its unspoilt parts, with their 'indescribable atmosphere of grace, of decayed and dusty elegance.' And from Valencia she wrote to Jean: 'Today . . . I had a much too eventful journey . . . a tyre went, and I had a terrible job changing the wheel, as when I had it jacked up the car moved back and upset the jack, and crashed down on its side, and I couldn't raise it without help of course. But a kind Spaniard from a passing *camion* stopped and helped me; it took ages, as my jack-handle broke, and he had to get his own jack, which was too tall, but at last, after an hour's hard labour in a broiling sun, we jacked it up again and changed the wheel. I said, when he lifted the car up by hand, that he was very strong. "Not very", he answered, "we don't get enough to eat", which was very sad and touching. Of course I gave him a large reward. I feel thankful that we all get the same amount in England, unlike here, where the rich get lots and the poor far too little, owing to *all* the food being sold at black-market prices.'

This incident of the broken jack was one of the last of Rose's mishaps on the roads of south-west Europe. By the first week of October she was in England again, having succeeded in covering nearly four thousand miles without any damage to herself.

16

AMONG THE RUINS

NEARLY TEN YEARS had passed since Rose had last written a novel. But in the spring of 1948, after her exhilarating travels in Spain and the enjoyment of writing *Fabled Shore*, she felt able to return to her 'popular' medium. 'I am writing a novel again', she told Gilbert Murray, with whom she was corresponding regularly. 'Rather a rest, after several books which needed mugging up, to sit about and spin fiction out of an uninformed mind. The kind of writing that can be gone on with in trains and buses, with no books at hand . . . I spent much of to-day in the ruins round St Paul's, which I like. The golden charlock and fennel luxuriate among . . . [the] catacombs and the broken cellars of what once were houses and offices. Part of my new novel is laid in this wrecked scene.' 'I am glad you are doing a novel', he replied. 'Novels are read more, and, if good, live longer than other books, and besides, I want to read another of yours.'

We know he thought highly of Rose's novels, and the phrase 'another of yours' suggests that he was anticipating the sort of book which most of Rose's readers meant when they said 'a new Rose Macaulay', in other words a witty satire. But her new book, *The World my Wilderness*, was to have more in common, as regards general tone, with *They Were Defeated* than with *Keeping up Appearances* or *Going Abroad*. Although no novel of Rose's could fail to contain light touches, *The World my Wilderness* was to be a deeply pessimistic book. When Rose wrote it she was looking unflinchingly at the wreckage left by the war, not only in terms of human habitations but of human lives.

The world my wilderness, its caves my home,
Its weedy wastes the garden where I roam,
Its chasm'd cliffs my castle and my tomb.[1]

The outstanding characteristic of *The World my Wilderness* is an all-embracing compassion. Rose's sufferings during the war years, far from embittering her, had deepened her capacity for understanding and pity. People of many kinds are shown in *The World my Wilderness*, old and young, rich and poor, conventional and bohemian, law-abiding and thieving, and each one of them is portrayed with tenderness, though without any trace of sentimentality. Especially is this so in the case of the central figure – one hesitates to call her a heroine, she is so far from heroic – a girl of seventeen called 'Barbary', the child of a broken home who in wartime France had drifted into the fringes of the maquis, with its lawlessness and betrayal and violence.

How fascinating that Rose, when in her late sixties she began afresh as a novelist, should have chosen as her main character a type who had appeared again and again in her earliest novels, a young person of childlike vulnerability who in one way or another has had to endure hard knocks. But the amiable waifs of the pre-1914 vintage, frail pathetic figures at odds with an alien world, were a far cry from the sullen, wary, defiant Barbary, whom Rose once described as 'rather lost and strayed and derelict'. Barbary stands for all the unhappy young of that era which began when the second war ended, the young who are forced to find their own level in a world which they discover to be corrupt, indifferent, merciless and utterly insecure. It is as though Rose, at the start of her career, had been making practice sketches in water-colour and pastel for the masterpiece she would one day, so long afterwards, create, the strong, subtle portrait of a precociously adult teenager whose life is in ruins.

Throughout the story of Barbary can be seen Rose's profound

[1] Epigraph composed by R.M.

concern for the decline in moral standards that had been steepening in Britain since the war, leaving its trail of distrust and misery, and undermining the uprightness which in her own generation had been taken for granted. At the start of the book, in the sunshine of a Mediterranean fishing village, Barbary's aberrant ways are disregarded by her mother, a hedonistic divorcée. But when she is sent, against her will, to live in ultra-respectable London, the context is very different. There her behaviour causes shock and concern. 'It's something rather new for people brought up like you to steal', she is told sternly after purloining the notecase of an elderly friend. Inevitably she breaks away, finding refuge among the ruins near St Paul's, then a meeting place for youthful drifters. These ruins, which held such a compelling attraction for Rose herself, as she wandered among them in the spring of 1948, symbolised for her, as she wrote *The World my Wilderness*, the contemporary chaos of disintegrating moral values, the chaos in which, although petty theft is still looked on askance, a whole gamut of fraud and deceit, from adultery to cheating the Customs, is regarded by the majority of the 'educated' as socially acceptable. Barbary's English half-brother, an intelligent, charming undergraduate, admits that he is a crook in a world of crooks.

The World my Wilderness, which was published in 1950, added greatly to Rose's stature as a novelist. In the view of one of her most discerning friends, William Plomer, it is the best novel she ever wrote, not just 'one of the best'. He gave this opinion after her death, so *The Towers of Trebizond* was included in his judgment. It is a book which invites rereading, demands it even. 'I missed the point dreadfully the first time. It is rather heartrending and frightening', Gilbert Murray confessed during his second reading. And a very perceptive friend of Rose's later observed, after reading the book for a third time, that only when one is familiar with the whole story is one's mind free to appreciate the masterly subtleties of characterisation and dialogue.[1] This same friend was one of the few to appreciate that the book possessed what Rose called 'a religious motif'.[2] By this she meant that throughout the story there runs a hidden theme attuned to eternity, the theme of sin and separation from God, and the resultant state of spiritual torment. In a sense, therefore, *The World my Wilderness* is a parable, but it includes one passage where the 'religious motif' emerges directly. In the ruins of a city church Barbary and her young French stepbrother (who like herself had run wild during the war) are about to enact a make-believe Mass to the accompaniment of jazz from a portable radio. Then a mad clergyman stumbles in (he had lost his reason during the Blitz, after being trapped for two days in the wreckage of a bombed church). He proceeds to recite the Anglican service of Holy Communion and then, standing where the pulpit had once been, he raves in terrifying terms of everlasting fire, of being trapped by sins from which there is no escape.

We are in hell now. Hell is where I am, Lucifer and all his legions are in me. Fire creeps on me from all sides; I am trapped in the prison of my sins; I cannot get out, there is no rescue possible, for I have shut myself from God in the hell of my own making. I cannot move my limbs, I cannot raise my hands to God, I cannot call to him from my place of darkness. The flames press on; they will consume my body, but my soul will live on in hell, for ever damned for I have turned from God and he must turn from me. O, the way's dark and horrid! I cannot see: shall I have no company? O yes, my sins; they run before me to fetch fire from hell. Trapped, trapped, trapped; there's no hope . . . The weight of my sins; they lie across my chest and pin me; I cannot stir. For this is hell, hell, hell.

In terms of Rose's own experience this nightmarish outburst

[1] Father Johnson, writing to C.B.S., 17 April 1959.
[2] *Letters to a Friend*, p. 50.

may of course be regarded as no more than a reflection of her wartime horror of being trapped alive, as well as perhaps an echo of childhood memories of Dante's *Inferno* and of her mother's teachings on hell fire. But in the light of her subsequent spiritual development it can be seen to possess a far deeper significance. When she put into words the anguish of the mad priest, she brought into the open the anguish of her own tormented conscience. Ever since she had proved incapable of breaking away from Gerald she had felt herself to be living in mortal sin, cut off from divine grace. On the surface, it is true, she had come to terms with her spiritual exile, but not long after *The World my Wilderness* was published she was to admit, with joy and thanksgiving, that the writing of it had been for her 'an unconscious prayer'.[1]

The theme of disintegration, not only in smashed and decaying buildings but in the evolution of countries and the lives of individuals, haunted Rose's mind, in one form or another, for many years. *The World my Wilderness* was not her first expression of it, nor her last. As early as 1930, in *Staying with Relations*, she had described the enjungled ruins of Guatemala; then she was able to treat them merely as evocative scenery. After her home was bombed, in 'Miss Anstruther's Letters', the smouldering ashes of a block of flats symbolised her own desolation. In *They Went to Portugal* an intellectual interest came to the fore, as she wrote of ruined Lisbon after the Great Earthquake. In *Fabled Shore* she linked past and present, historical and aesthetic, as she pondered on the harsh and splendid ruins of Spain. Next came *The World my Wilderness*. And then finally she wrote the book which was to represent the culmination of her obsessive concern with ruins and all they stood for, *Pleasure of Ruins*, to which she devoted four years of arduous work. Her aim was an ambitious one. She set out not merely to tell of the various ruins that had given her pleasure,

[1] *Letters to a Friend*, p. 292.

but to show the ways in which men of all eras, all over the world, had reacted to ruins, whether in grief or melancholy, in vindictive triumph, in nostalgia or in aesthetic delight.

The word 'pleasure' in the title is of great significance. For although Rose's labours on the book were often back-breaking and although during those four years she was often held up by illness, it was while writing *Pleasure of Ruins* that she gradually came to recover the zest of her earlier 'pleasure books' (*The Minor Pleasures of Life* and *Personal Pleasures*) and much of the magnificent prose in *Pleasure of Ruins* has a lyrical ring that tells of a lightened heart.

In the first place, when Rose started on '*Ruins*' in the summer of 1949, immediately after finishing *The World my Wilderness*, it was not intended to be a lengthy work: Weidenfeld and Nicolson, who had invited her to contribute to their series 'Pleasures and Treasures', had asked for a book of not more than 40,000 words. But by the time she had been working on 'The Pleasures of Looking at Ruins' for about a year she was manifestly outstripping the 'Pleasures and Treasures' category. Nigel Nicolson, looking back to this time, has commented from the publisher's angle: 'It soon became clear that it would be a pity to throw away Rose and the subject on such a trivial production, so the book grew. From time to time, when I saw her, she would apologise for the fact that the book was expanding far beyond the first concept, and of course we were only too delighted.'

The first years of Rose's work on *Pleasure of Ruins*, between 1949 and 1951, were the years when her friendship with Gilbert Murray blossomed. It was a friendship which meant a great deal to both of them. He on his side obviously came to count on her as a sympathetic and stimulating confidante, while on Rose's side affection was mixed with reverence. For him she had been 'Dear Rose' almost from the first, but for her he long remained 'Dear Professor Murray'. When eventually, just after *Pleasure of Ruins* was published, she began to address him as 'Dear Gilbert' she added at once 'I did ask leave for this, and hope it is all right!'

Just how often they exchanged letters at this time is not certain, for there are manifest gaps in the surviving correspondence, but it is clear that they kept closely in touch by letter and also met whenever they could. Gilbert Murray, though by now nearly 85 and easily fatigued, still came frequently to London, and he and Rose sometimes had a meal together at the Athenaeum. Alternatively he might look in at Hinde House for a morning chat, or join her for tea at a small café in Spring Street near Paddington Station before catching a train back to Oxford.

Their letters show that they enjoyed discussing a great variety of subjects. On a personal level they took an intimate interest in one another's ailments and domestic troubles, and also shared in any excitements such as Rose's being given an Honorary Doctorate of Letters by Cambridge University in 1951. They constantly exchanged news of their many friends, and also liked comparing notes on broadcasts (Rose was taking part at this time in the BBC 'Critics' programme). Politics at home and abroad were a frequent topic; both felt themselves to be unwavering Liberals, however dim the prospects of Liberalism, and Rose's loyalty to the spirit of the League of Nations was in step with his. Together, as the Cold War became colder, they mourned the worsening fortunes of the United Nations, pondered upon the Communist threat, and shuddered over Korea. It was as though the two friends, the aged philosopher and his disciple, were comparing their impressions as they paced side by side through the ruins of the devastated world.

Rose gladly took advantage of being able to discuss her researches for *Pleasure of Ruins* with such an eminent scholar, and the interest of a man whom she respected so much was a stimulus to the whole enterprise. She did, in fact, intend to 'honour her book' by dedicating it to him, but unfortunately failed to mention this to her publishers until too late. Often she turned to him for an opinion. 'What would you say were among the earliest Greek appreciations of ancient ruins?' she asked in one of her letters. 'They didn't, of course, mostly see the Babylonish ones – Nineveh, Babylon, etc. (though Xenophon describes Nineveh ruins, I think). There was Crete, of course . . . Strabo relates of some . . . But was there much real interest in antique ruins as such, I wonder? It is always difficult to distinguish interest in antique remains from interest in what they had once been. Pausanias is usually rather cursory and Baedekerish about them; no wonder, considering how much he had to get through.'

In another of her letters she consulted him about Rome: 'I simply can't believe that the Christian pilgrims, who expressed nothing but interest in the churches and relics they had come to see for their souls' sake, didn't really stop and gape at the pagan monuments. In fact, according to Bede, the English [pilgrims] . . . originated the saying "If the Colosseum falls, Rome will fall, and with Rome the world", only they said it of course in Latin. So, by the eighth century, they must have been taking some interest in pagan buildings.'

Most of Rose's work on her vast subject was carried out in libraries and at home. But she made quite a few expeditions to see interesting ruins with her own eyes. Usually she tried to fit in some bathing as well, for though now nearly seventy, swimming was more than ever a favourite pleasure (at about this time she took to swimming in London, both in the Serpentine and at the Lansdowne Club). Thus in the summer of 1949, when she went on a ruin-hunt to Ireland, it was partly to try the bathing. But in this case there was also an additional motive. According to Marjorie Grant Cook, who accompanied her, the trip was secretly a kind of pilgrimage, for Rose wanted to visit Loughrea, the Galway parish where Gerald had once been a priest. Sometimes she was unduly optimistic about the likelihood of bathing weather. In the following spring she was apparently hoping for some Atlantic bathing at Eastertime, when she went to Wales to

see the artificial ruins that Clough Williams-Ellis had put up in
his grounds at Portmeirion.

She was, needless to say, longing to travel much farther afield.
'How I should like to see Palmyra, Baalbek, Rhodes, Cyprus,
Syria, India, and South America, as well as all the Greek islands',
she exclaimed to Gilbert Murray, '[and] I want to see the sub-
marine ruins off the Salamis coast, and dive among them. They
say this can be done.' In the summer of 1950 she did go abroad, to
Italy, and visited a few ruins, but the holiday was chiefly memorable for the bathing. She learnt to swim underwater, equipped
with 'one of those lovely goggle masks with air-pipes . . . you get
such a nice view of the fishes and sea-weed grottos.'[1] There was
however one disappointment. She found herself agreeing with
Cicero that the bays of Naples and Salerno were far too populous.
'All the coasts get denser year by year. Where will it end?'

The freedom that her publishers were giving her as regards the
length and scope of her book was in some ways a joy; at one point
she felt relaxed enough to write some poems on the theme of
ruins, quite aside from her book. But by the spring of 1951 – she
was by this time 'wrestling with Persian and Indian palaces' – she
had to admit that 'all these ruins' were getting her down. That
year she did not go abroad, instead she joined Jean and Nancy
Willetts on the Isle of Wight, 'this delightful Victorian island',
with its 'peculiar tranquil charm' (in subsequent years she returned
there several times). Then early in 1952 she became quite seriously
ill. Each year, as she grew older, she succumbed to influenza or
bronchial troubles,[2] but this time it was another 'most tedious
disease' namely undulant fever. For months it nagged at her
intermittently, and not until the end of the year had she finally
thrown it off.

Yet somehow, with undefeatable persistence, she had been

[1] *Letters to a Friend*, p. 68.
[2] R.M. liked to imagine that she looked after herself when ill. In fact Jean and
Nancy Willetts often took it in turns to come up from Romford to nurse her.

working at '*Ruins*' in spite of her illness, and as 1953 began she was in the 'final throes' of her book, 'having a terrific tussle with ruined cities of India and Ceylon'. 'This wretched book devours me, body and soul', she told Gilbert Murray. 'I toil day and night, only snatching odd hours off for food . . . funerals . . . etc. All, or nearly all, correspondence I ignore (not with you, for that is a Treat).' There was however a consoling prospect ahead. In mid-May, by which time, she felt sure, she would have finished her book, she was going abroad, first to Cyprus and then to the Levant. The holiday fulfilled her hopes. 'I saw some wonderful things in Jordan and Syria and Palestine', she wrote to Gilbert Murray on her return. 'Gerasa is being wonderfully reconstructed. Caesarea was very magnificent in its desolation on the coast – nearly all vanished, but with the ghost of the great Roman pleasure-city whispering about the port. I was interested in Israel, and explored a good deal of it – the coast, from Tortosa down to Askelon, Tiberias and Galilee, etc. I bathed in the Dead Sea (*On* it, I should say, for one sits upright, clasping one's knees).'

When *Pleasure of Ruins* was published, in December 1953, Rose was hopeful about its prospects, though she evidently felt she must be prepared for disappointments. 'A book like that doesn't expect large sales', she wrote to a friend just after it was out.[1] 'It will cost 25/-, which, as it is large, illustrated, and nicely produced, isn't expensive at current prices . . . [It] has had, so far, a very nice kind press . . . I am surprised and relieved, having got myself rather tired of the book, to find that people do, apparently, like it.' One of the people who liked it, who indeed rhapsodised over it, was Gilbert Murray.

I read Ruins in the train all the way to Oxford, with the result that my eyes almost refuse to read at all. It is a lovely book. I never could quite make out what it was going to be about, but now I see. The stupendous Past and the transience

[1] *Last Letters to a Friend*, p. 126.

of everything – Ozymandias, king of kings, in fact. But what massive learning you show! Of course I know nothing of your 17th and 18th century travellers, that is all normal; but you know Suetonius and Pliny and suchlike. I can only murmur sulkingly that anyhow they are not Greek. I like the 'windy words' of the Hebrew prophets and the 'storm-ridden conscience' of Christianity. And how moving is all the bit about the false Troys which stirred people so much. I haven't read more than a third of the book, but I see what a heartless waste was left by the dissolution of the monasteries, and also of how our feeling is changed, and, I think, deepened, by the new ruins.

A fortnight later he wrote again. 'Your learning overwhelms me. I can't think how you amassed all your stuff.' To which Rose replied very simply: 'I *am* glad you like my book which is really dedicated to you.'

17

REORIENTATION

AT FIRST GLANCE it might seem that Rose's life at the age of seventy[1] was running busily on without any notable changes of direction or tempo. Her stamina was hardly diminished and she was as energetic as ever; even in the thick of *Pleasure of Ruins* she kept in touch with her friends and relations, and managed to find time for occasional articles and broadcasts. Meantime she still liked to indulge in many of the activities of her youth, and not only swam as often as possible but bicycled and went for long walks, rowed (gently) when occasion offered, and even, when 'in lonely and unobserved country', climbed trees.

Behind the scenes however, at first unknown even to Jean, and never so much as hinted at to her friends, a fundamental change was beginning to take place in her as she approached her seventieth birthday. The tenor of her secret, inner life, long one of despairing pessimism, was being gradually transformed into one of serenity and hope. The heartcry of *The World my Wilderness*, the 'unconscious prayer' for forgiveness and reintegration, was little by little being answered.

The fact that this metamorphosis took place, and that in time it shaped the remainder of her life at every level, kindling the happiness which during her last years was so evident to those around her, is already widely known. For the two books of her letters to Father Johnson, *Letters to a Friend* and *Last Letters to a Friend*, which were published ten years ago, showed with moving clarity and in her own words the course it took and the effects it

[1] She was seventy on 1 August 1951.

Rose during a cruise to Turkey and the Aegean, 1958

Dame Rose Macaulay

had. But there has not hitherto been an opportunity to view it in the context of her whole life, and the present book provides a timely chance to show it in longer perspective.

It all began when Rose arrived home from Italy in August 1950 (after the holiday when she learnt to swim under water) and found awaiting her an unexpected letter from Cambridge, Mass. Father Johnson, now aged 73, had felt suddenly prompted to write and tell her how much he had enjoyed a recent reading of *They Were Defeated*. He reminded her that he had long ago been her confessor – they had been out of touch for nearly thirty-five years – and that during the First World War she had been to a retreat he conducted. He also told her that he sometimes remembered her in his prayers.

For Rose, who was in a state of 'darkness and tension and struggle' (so she later told him) what a supremely heartening letter! Father Johnson knew nothing of her long years of 'living in mortal sin', of her self-imposed excommunication; he had written to her as though to the woman he had known and cared for pastorally before she had ever met Gerald O'Donovan. Here then, extended to her gratuitously, was an unspoken invitation, a most auspicious opportunity, to renew contact with a spiritual guide whom she liked and trusted. 'If you were in England', she wrote back, 'I should probably ask if I might come and talk to you sometimes, and I wish you were. I remember that Retreat so well . . . [and] how much what you said helped and stimulated me . . . I kept notes of it for many years . . . [Your addresses] had impressed me very much; they were about prayer, and goodness, and not getting separated from God. I remember I came away resolved to try to be good for ever . . . It is now very many years since I went to a Retreat or anything at all of that nature; I have sadly lost touch with that side of life, and regret it. We do need it so badly, in this queer world and life, all going to pieces and losing. Most of my younger friends have never had it, and haven't, therefore, that ultimate sanction for goodness, unselfishness, integrity, kindness, self-denial, which those brought up to believe in God accept at any rate as ideals, even if they have lost the belief... Please go on occasionally remembering me when you think of it, for I value that extremely... Do write again some time.' Father Johnson wrote again at once and continued to write, while Rose herself replied eagerly, and thus began the friendship by letter which was to have such beneficent and far-reaching effects.

Father Johnson's letters to Rose are no longer in existence: they were among the personal papers which in accordance with her overall instructions were destroyed after her death. But we can tell something of their flavour from her descriptions of them. 'Your letters are (from any standpoint) so good', she wrote to him when they had been corresponding for just over six months. 'They have every quality – range, depth, breadth, humour, wisdom, interest, sympathy, even (I like to think) affection.' And later she exclaimed 'Goodness, what I owe to them! No one can ever have had such letters. Your patience with me, your making clear to me so much that was obscure or that I had never thought of, your bringing me into touch with the Church, with the sacraments, with the whole marvel of reconciliation and the newness of this new life in which I have tried to live, however faultily, for nearly five years now – well, I don't need to tell you all this, for you know it. It has been the most wonderful ministry of letters that ever was.'

As a record of Rose's return to Christian practice, and to a state of spiritual equilibrium, her own side of the correspondence is historically of much importance. For in spite of all the evidence to the contrary, some have persisted in believing that throughout the latter part of her life she remained outside the Church, a critical agnostic. Over and above this however her letters are of unique value for the insights they give into her character; when she wrote to Father Johnson she wrote with absolute honesty.

None of her letters to other people, fascinating and revealing as some of them are, can compare as regards showing us 'the real Rose'. Beside them the correspondence with Gilbert Murray seems like a tea-party conversation, while the letters to Jean, for all their fun and their charm, are as full of reticence as of sisterly chat. The fact that Father Johnson had once been her confessor meant that there was no need whatever to keep up appearances; all preliminary hedging could be dispensed with as well as all posing. Writing to him about her spiritual problems, or indeed about anything else, she obviously felt as free as if she were discussing her health with a trusted doctor. She herself was thankfully aware of this: 'People don't think I am shy, because I gabble away to anyone about anything or nothing; but that's different . . . I believe there is no one but you to whom I find it easy to talk (or write) on the subjects I have written to you about. To you it is entirely easy and natural. Partly it is that you have always met me half-way, or more than half-way, and one has the feeling that you really care. Then, you understand all I say or ask, with all its implications and overtones, and your answers always cover what I meant and add more to it; and I always understand what you mean. Incidentally, you have a knack, which pleases me, of making me laugh a little even on a serious subject.'

When they first started writing she was somewhat diffident. 'I mustn't bother you . . . one should consume one's own smoke.' But within a short time her scruples dropped away, and after only a few exchanges she was able to open her heart to him. Before the end of 1950 she had brought repentantly into the open, of her own accord, her long-buried burden of guilt, and his response was so comforting that within a matter of weeks she was returning to sacramental confession and then to Holy Communion. It was not, at first, an easy path and the pangs of contrition were painful. But Father Johnson's support was sensitive and gentle as well as strong. He also helped her in dealing with her 'doubts'; there were various Christian doctrines which she felt she could not accept (the Resurrection, as she understood it, was one of them). Here he agreed that she must not strain after 'belief'; rather she must leave her doubts on one side for the time being, concentrating instead upon the eucharistic worship which came easily to her. Before long the Eucharist was the central focus of all her devotion; 'I value the contact with God through the Sacrament more than anything in the world.' And already after Holy Week 1951 she could write, 'I felt, at the Easter Mass, that here was Christ risen and with us, and I didn't care how.' She was obviously pleased to find that some of her new reactions coincided with those of Father Johnson himself: 'Yes, isn't it a wonderful corporate feeling of being carried along, being part of the body, not looking at it from outside, from beyond a fence. And, as you say, everything in it fits gradually in, forming the pattern of the whole; and the bits one doesn't yet grasp, or that don't mean anything much to one, may one day [come to do so]. Anyhow that doesn't matter [in relation] to the whole pattern and movement in which one is involved . . . [it is like] a great sweeping symphony that one can hear a little of the meaning of now and then.' Many of the 'bits' did fall into place for Rose, but some years later she admitted that some of them still did not. 'You know . . . there are and always have been a lot of things I can't and don't try to accept; I just can't feel they matter, and don't strain after them. I have God, Christ, the Holy Spirit, and the Mass; the rest I don't concern myself with, except as the ancient idiom which enshrines these central things for me . . . Anyhow . . . minds are so different, and must work on things in their own way, and God will make allowance for our limitations . . . *O Sapientia:* we must pray that she will lead us all along the road.'

Less than a year after Father Johnson's momentous fan-letter Rose was established as a regular worshipper, both on Sundays and through the week, at the Grosvenor Chapel in South Audley Street. This small eighteenth-century church was conveniently within reach of Hinde House, and its special brand of Anglicanism

– high but not 'extreme' – seemed to Rose perfection. '*What* a heritage we have', she exclaimed to her 'non-resident chaplain', 'I mean, we Anglicans. It is so incredibly beautiful . . . our particular ceremonial and dignity without fuss.' Time and again she repeated how glad she was to be back. Even during her lapsed period, she said, she had always felt herself an Anglican – an '*Anglo*-agnostic' and an 'Anglo-non-church-goer'. It was 'a matter of taste and affection, and perhaps a kind of loyalty, rather than of belief . . . a kind of spiritual capital, laid up for one by one's ancestors and upbringing, and by various influences since. Certainly no merit of mine.'

At this stage she was discovering how much she valued the Book of Common Prayer. Many of the collects, in particular, were very dear to her; they had been imprinted on her memory as a child. But her love for the Prayer Book was not merely sentimental; with her appreciation of good English she treasured the dignified Anglican prose. 'There is much in R.C. devotions that I can't stomach', she told Father Johnson, '*Nothing* in what a contemptuous convert called "Cranmer's little work".' She had reservations, too, about extempore prayer. 'The *words* of liturgies can carry us, even without very strong feeling, in a way extempore prayer can't.' But her enthusiasm for well-composed prayers was not confined to Cranmer or to the English language. With help and encouragement from Father Johnson, a practised Latinist, she gradually compiled a collection of the prayers she liked best, both in Latin and English, and transcribed them, along with various texts, fragments of poetry etc. into a little book that Father Johnson himself had made for her (book-binding was one of his hobbies). She kept this green booklet in her handbag, and obviously turned often to her *Preces Privatae*, as she called it, for its pages are worn with use.

In the old days Rose and Father Johnson had never been personal friends; they had met only as penitent and confessor. But as soon as they started corresponding they discovered so many interests in common, secular as well as religious, and it seemed so natural to share them, that they might almost have been friends since childhood. So it seemed very appropriate when, after getting to know one another for about eighteen months, they discovered to their mutual joy that they were fourth cousins. This establishing of a family link coincided with a change in the tone of Rose's letters. By now she had a regular confessor in London, so Father Johnson was no longer her only spiritual guide. She remained as profoundly grateful to him as ever, and continued to write once or twice a week, with obvious enjoyment and at considerable length, but from now on he was not only a respected adviser. He was her dear cousin Hamilton, with whom she felt entirely at ease, who took an intense and affectionate interest in all her doings, and who like herself doted on discussing religious matters.

Rose was by now making friends among her fellow Anglicans, and although she still counted on seeing her agnostic friends as usual, she found herself giving more and more time to those with whom she shared her faith. At first her two lives did not mix easily. 'Oh dear', she lamented to Father Johnson, after she had accepted, without a thought, an invitation from the Stephen Spenders to a dinner party on Ash Wednesday, 'this living life in two such different climates is complicated, and I don't do it well. One is too much entangled in one's past, and bogged in its ways.'

A new friend whom Rose saw often, for she worshipped at Grosvenor Chapel, was Susan Lister,[1] 'a very able theological lecturer at King's College London . . . a delightful person . . . and a very strong Anglican.'[2] Another was Canon Frederic Hood; she often gave him a lift to Grosvenor Chapel when he was due to officiate there. 'No company . . . interests me more (just now) than that of the intelligent clergy, and I like to discuss things

[1] Now Mrs Mark Hodson.
[2] R.M. to Dorothea Conybeare, 19 September 1956.

with them when we meet, and they are interested, I think, to do this . . . I must try and be a go-between, in a slight way, between the clergy I know and the intelligent laity.' Two other Anglican clergy who became friends of Rose's at this time were Patrick McLaughlin, vicar of St Thomas's Regent Street, and the young assistant priest there, Gerard Irvine, whom she described to Father Johnson as 'a rather new type to me; very social, I expect rather worldly, and very extreme'. She enjoyed joking with Gerard Irvine about the 'Romanist' practices at St Thomas's and else-where; nevertheless she did not feel happy on the rare occasions when she took part in such worship, and returned to Grosvenor Chapel with a sigh of relief. There the High Church ritual was, to her mind, not exaggerated but just right, and 'all very nice and Anglican'.

It was at the beginning of 1953, when Rose was at last finishing *Pleasure of Ruins*, that her new allegiance to the Anglican Church became generally known amongst her friends and acquaintances, to the rejoicing of some and the dismay of others. With T. S. Eliot it was of course a bond. Less predictably she received warm congratulations from a friend who was a Roman Catholic. 'Lord Pakenham',[1] she told Jean, 'who always tries to convert me . . . said he had been delighted to hear that I was now a practising Anglican, which was big of him. I fancy he thinks it is [a] step nearer Rome.' An old acquaintance, Lady Mander, on the other hand, telephoned to ask whether it could possibly be true that Rose had become an Anglo-Catholic. 'She had always looked on me as "a staunch agnostic" like herself', Rose told Dorothea Conybeare; 'I answered that I do now go to church sometimes, though I didn't before (not for a long time, that is) and she was much surprised and rather disappointed in me.'

Inevitably there were certain cases where the reorientation of Rose's inner life brought with it a decline in a long-established

[1] Now Lord Longford.

relationship. Dorothy Brooke, by now Lady Nicholson,[1] later admitted that she and Rose 'lost touch rather' after Rose became 'so wrapped up in her religious life'. Victor Gollancz was another who found her new attitude a barrier; in *Reminiscences of Affection* he wrote as follows: 'During her last years something happened between us. There was no hint of a breach . . . but the old careless days, when we had adored her and she had adored us, were over . . . Perhaps . . . the more integral practice of her religion . . . led to a certain lessening of her intimacy with, a certain withdrawal from, ourselves and maybe others.'

One friend of long standing with whom Rose remained on cordial terms, while accepting with regret the intransigence of his anti-Christian convictions, was E. M. Forster. And Forster himself, so he told his biographer Nicholas Furbank, became increasingly fond of Rose towards the end of her life. 'When she was younger she was a bit arrogant', he said. 'She got nicer as she got older.' This change for the better in Rose's character was even more evident to someone who saw her far more often than Forster, namely Jean. 'After her "conversion" Rose became gentler, softer', is how she puts it, 'and she didn't say such spiteful things any more.' It was a joy to Jean (whose own faith had never wavered) to be able to look forward wholeheartedly to Rose's weekly visits to Romford: previously, although she always loved seeing her, she had in a sense dreaded them, for Rose often sneered at religion in a way that distressed her – it had wounded Margaret too. Now, in the mid-1950s, the two sisters came to count on one another more and more. Since 1952, when Eleanor died in India they were the only two left of all the Macaulay family.[2] 'The way one's family founders is dreadful, one gets to feel like a survivor

[1] She had married Sir Walter Nicholson in 1939, two years after the death of her first husband.

[2] Eleanor died suddenly after a heart attack, at the age of 65, on 5 August 1952. During the latter part of her life her missionary work at Chota Nagpur had included the translating of religious writings into Hindi, at which she excelled.

from a wreck', Rose wrote to a bereaved friend[1] at the time of
Eleanor's death.

Another result of Rose's 'more integral practice of her religion
was that she began to take a serious interest in her godchildren
especially Mary Anne O'Donovan. Towards the end of 1953 she
wrote to Father Johnson: 'Did I ever tell you of my little goddaughter Mary Anne, now 12? I sponsored her at a time when (I
now see) I was in no fit state to be sponsoring anyone – but there
it is, I *am* her godmother, and I did promise to see that she was
brought up a Christian.' So she started taking Mary Anne and her
young sister Jane to the children's services at St Mary Abbots, and
then out to tea afterwards, and helped them to learn the Prayer
Book catechism. 'Perhaps I made a mistake in telling them that the
proper answer to "What did your godfathers and godmothers
then for you?" was "Silver mug, spoon and fork"; this joke
stuck, and I fear I shall get this answer only. I remember we used
to think it funny! . . . Mary Anne told me at tea that they didn't
believe anything yet but that later on she thought of becoming a
Roman Catholic. I said "You'll have to believe plenty if you do
that, you know", to which she replied, "No, I shan't believe it.
But I like the churches, and they have prayers in Latin." She has
begun Latin at school, and likes it.'

Henceforward Rose shared in many of the doings of her 'two
little girls' and even (in 1955) accompanied them to the Butlin's
Camp at Skegness for a week's holiday. 'Butlin's was quite fun',
she wrote to Father Johnson afterwards. 'Rather like a visit to the
moon, quite out of this world. Absurd, of course, for an adult,
but having the two children made it fun; they loved every minute
of it . . . We all slept in nice little chalets in a row, or rather in
many rows, for there were about 500 campers at a time. We had
swimming pools (but I bathed in the sea myself) and every kind
of game and diversion, and my younger charge, who is pony-
mad, rode every day and helped to groom the horses. There was

[1] Marjorie Grant Cook.

a repertory company, which acted exciting drama, and television, which I saw for the first time and didn't think much of. Why is it so popular? One programme, which showed a panel of 4 famous people in a game of guessing "Who wrote that?" to my surprise quoted something from me (but I don't know where I said it) – something about "it is to the eccentrics that the world owes most of its knowledge"; no one guessed me; when they were told, they had to discuss its truth or otherwise, and on the whole they agreed with me. My two children were delighted by this.'

18

TREBIZOND

'TREBIZOND stands . . . not merely [for] the actual city (though this comes in, and a lovely place it is) but for the . . . romantic and nostalgic vision of the Church which haunts the person who narrates the story.' Thus Rose explained to Father Johnson the essence of her new novel, *The Towers of Trebizond*, when she wrote in February 1956 to tell him it was just completed. She was now seventy-four, and five years had passed since she began again as a Christian; when she wrote *The Towers of Trebizond* she had left behind her the difficult initial stages of contrition and readjustment. She now felt, with joy, that she really belonged within what she called in her epigraph 'that strange bright city'. And she could now perceive with alarming awareness that the Eternal City, for which man has an undying hunger, is barred to all those 'who do not desire to enter it more strongly than they desire all other cities', those who by their own choice remain stubbornly within 'cities' which are illusory and transient. Rose could not have written *Trebizond* while she still felt herself an exile. But she was now strongly enough rooted in the Church to express a burning longing to help others, by sharing with them – so far as she could – her own experience of a divided life, and of what, in spiritual terms, it had cost her.

In *The Towers of Trebizond* her talent for combining a serious message with light satire flowered to its fullest, as she wove together tragedy and comedy, fantasy and farce. But her sense of humour sparkled so brightly that quite a few people failed to appreciate the book's more heartfelt aspects. Rose was astonished and dismayed when she heard (through one of her cousins, Lady Fletcher) that someone had thought the whole thing was 'a leg-pull'. 'Never was a novel (by me) more passionately in earnest (I mean in its religious and moral parts)' she protested. 'I wrote it in a kind of white-hot passion; but perhaps made too many jokes as well, which confused the issue to many readers. [What] I hope . . . most people saw in it [was] . . . the struggle of good and evil in the human soul, and its eternal importance, and the pull and power of the Christian Church on the divided mind, its torment and its attraction.'

Rose herself had seen Trebizond in the summer of 1954, when for the first time she visited Turkey. She made the trip alone and it was an exciting but very exhausting one; she had not reckoned with the blazing heat. Before she came home she had succumbed more than once to what she called 'Turkey fever' and had been miserably ill. But the early part of her travels, when she journeyed along the Black Sea coast, was a delight and an inspiration. She was disappointed to find that it was out of the question, according to Turkish ideas, for a woman to bathe in the Black Sea, but at Trebizond – 'the last little Byzantine empire' – she was able to wander alone up the hills behind the town, to the overgrown ruins of the ancient citadel, and it was this melancholy Byzantine Trebizond, its beauty mouldering under the barbarian yoke, that enchanted her more than anything else in Turkey.

In her novel the narrator 'Laurie' also wandered out from Trebizond to the ruined citadel, and here as so often in the book Laurie and Rose seem almost to coincide: this impression is heightened by the narrator's use of the first person. Rose had never previously written a novel in the first person, and she purposely adopted a style that was not her own, so as to put the story 'at one remove' from herself. But her voice can often be heard in Laurie's chatter; her thinking can be traced in Laurie's ruminations. She amused herself by trying to keep her readers guessing as to whether Laurie was a man or a woman: 'so much of life is common to both sexes.' Often in the past she had chosen sexually ambiguous names for her main characters – Cecil, Julian, Evelyn, and many more – but not until *Trebizond* had she made the sex of her central figure a deliberate secret until the end of the book. Yet could anyone really have taken Laurie for a man? The narrator's 'rather goofy, rambling prose style' (as Rose herself called it) is essentially feminine, not masculine, in flavour, as also is the psychology behind it. Perhaps the most striking example of this is when Laurie, who is enmeshed in an adulterous love affair with her cousin Vere, ponders upon the contradictions of her love.

And then I thought how odd it was, all that love and joy and peace that flooded over me when I thought about Vere, and how it all came from what was a deep meanness in our lives, for that is what adultery is, a meanness and a stealing, a taking away from someone what should be theirs, a great selfishness and surrounded and guarded by lies lest it should be found out. And out of this meanness and this selfishness and this lying flow love and joy and peace, beyond anything that can be imagined. And this makes a discord in the mind, the happiness and the guilt and the remorse pulling in opposite ways so that the mind and soul are torn in two, and if it goes on for years and years the discord becomes permanent, so that it will never stop, and even if one goes on living after death, as some people think, there will still be this deep discord that nothing can heal, because of the great meanness and selfishness that caused such a deep joy. And there is no way out of this dilemma that I know.

When Rose had delivered her manuscript to Collins she wrote jubilantly to Father Johnson: 'Mark Bonham Carter, the director there who is my friend . . . likes it, I am glad to say. He read the beginning of it to his mother (Lady Violet B.C.) and he said it made her laugh, also him; he says he was also moved, so that is a good combination, I suppose – laughter and being moved.' She did not drop any hints to Father Johnson as to why her novel had evoked laughter, though in a letter to Gilbert Murray (with whom she was still corresponding, though now less often) she confided that it was concerned with 'some Turkey travel . . . and some Turks and Greeks and religious Anglicans and a mentally deranged camel and a precocious ape who learns to play chess and croquet and drive a car, and two British who vanish into Russia, and a lot of people all writing their books about Turkey.' Father Johnson, Rose was afraid, might not care for some of her 'irreverent' jokes – she had poked fun at 'extreme' clergy and showed the ape being taken to church, where it imitated some of the ritual. But she need not have worried. When later he read the book he was not in the least shocked, for he understood, with typical sensitivity, the thinking behind her satire. His only criticism, so it seems, concerned the note of hopelessness on which the story ended: Laurie, after the death of her lover in an accident when she herself was driving, feels irrevocably excluded from the heavenly city. But Rose stood her ground. 'I too, you know, felt Laurie's half-stunned insensibility, and even aversion, towards the Church, for some time after the man I had loved for so long died. I don't take Laurie far enough in her life to get to where she, as I did, encounters some influence that brings her church-ward. But of course it came; feeling as she always had about the Church and about separation from God, she would not for very long be outside it.' The same point about the ending was raised by another of Rose's friends, who asked whether Laurie might not have progressed to a stage where she would no longer have felt herself banished. 'I expect Laurie did later learn more about Christian love and Christian life, and get right inside the Church at last', Rose replied. 'Perhaps I'll write a sequel.'

'MAD CAMEL PLAYS A BIG PART IN UNUSUAL BOOK': this headline filled Rose with glee, and she felt happy, so she told

Jean, that there was 'something for everyone' in her book. But
during the first few weeks after publication she was on tenter-
hooks. Some of her letters to Dorothea Conybeare, to whom she
was now writing often, show how concerned she was as to
whether reviewers and readers would react favourably. 'I have
had only a few reviews so far, of course', she wrote when the book
was just out, 'of which the *Observer* was the best, and someone in
the *Manchester Guardian* the worst; she [Anne Duchene] found
the style "suffocatingly pert" . . . [and] Laurie "lethally self
conscious". I don't know how much she had grasped of the
book's theme; she didn't mention religion, or conscience, and
called it "a comedy" . . . All the other reviews have been nice,
though I think the *Evening Standard* ought not to have told the
story . . . but reviewers will do that . . . The best was by C. V.
Wedgwood in *Time and Tide* yesterday; it was long, and very
understanding.'

Dorothea was fascinated by the book. But another of Rose's
cousins, her sister Alison McCormick, did not care for it at all,
and thought the state of Laurie's emotions 'too complicated'. 'I
am sorry Alison dislikes the book', Rose commented. 'I find that
the clergy and other strong Anglicans mostly like it very much . . .
John Betjeman gave it a wonderful review in the *Telegraph* . . .
The only people so far (there may be plenty to come) who agree
with Alison in disliking it are two Roman Catholics . . . [the]
woman in the *Manchester Guardian* . . . and Sean O'Faolain in the
Listener, who simply hated it, and was thoroughly bored . . .
Otherwise, I think I have never had such a good press or so many
nice letters about a book. Still, everyone can't like it.'

She had been ready for disapproving notices in the Catholic
press, for she had made some outspoken criticisms of the Roman
Church, but to her surprise the *Tablet* was not unsympathetic.
'Christopher Hollis wrote an interesting and kind review. He
said it would be unfair to identify Laurie's views on religion etc.
and her comments on church history, with my own. Actually

they are all my own, I think; I mean . . . the criticisms . . . [of] its past cruelties and stupidities and narrowness of human failures . . . and . . . the admiration . . . [for] the spell and the beauty and the hold it has always had on imagination.' A few less intelligent Catholics, however, wrote letters to Rose that were adverse and also fanciful. 'The latest allegory', she told Dorothea, 'was from an R.C. who wanted to know if I had meant by the camel the exclusive and scornful Roman Church, and by the ape the C of E which apes Rome but never understands religion at all. I thought it a foolish question, as I was most unlikely to regard the C of E like that! She didn't like the book; she thought it absurd to boost the C of E as if it was a real Church with real sacraments etc., which could influence peoples' lives. They are very fractious and touchy about it on the whole, though not nearly all. Converts are the worst.'

By way of contrast many Anglicans, and also many would-be believers, responded to *Trebizond* in a manner which to Rose was profoundly moving. Some weeks after the book was out she wrote to tell Jean that she was beginning to feel 'almost like a priest', for so many people were telling her how much she had helped them in their religion. One friend, whom she described as 'agnostic, but wistfully religious', had written, 'That a person of your distinction and your entourage should affirm publicly, in August 1956, that she believes there is such a thing as sin, and that she is agin it, must hearten many also-rans who have had a suspicion all along that this might indeed be so. It will enliven their endeavours.' Another letter which Rose quoted to Father Johnson – it had touched her greatly – was from a friend who had had 'a storm-tossed emotional life, with several successive husbands and lovers.' She had told Rose that *Trebizond* would henceforth be her Bible: 'It is the most *improving* novel in my lifetime.' 'That is nonsense, of course', Rose added, 'and I only repeat it because I thought you might like to hear it said of a book by your daughter-in-God, for that I really am, you know.'

Appreciative letters also came from friends who were 'known unbelievers'; Julian Huxley wrote 'One realises that there must be an institution like the Church, to enshrine peoples' religious and moral values.' But Gilbert Murray, so Rose told Dorothea, who had started on *Trebizond* 'to cheer himself after his wife's death', had confessed that he 'did not understand' the book. Yet he warmed to it when he read it a second time, shortly before his own death. 'I was pricked on to . . . read [it] again', he wrote to Rose, 'by hearing someone say that when she read the first sentence "Take my camel, dear" she burst out laughing. So I have read it again and seen what hundreds of things I had simply missed at my first reading – missed through sheer stupidity in me, or unexpectedness in them. I also feel how deeply moving it is, with its contrast of the things that just happen to you and the things that permanently matter.' Rose in her reply showed how overjoyed she was by his second thoughts, but added, 'I don't know why people laugh at "Take my camel, dear." It seems to me such a natural remark to make on returning home from a camel ride.' The popularity of the *Trebizond* camel was proving something of a burden to Rose. Towards the end of 1956 she wrote to a goddaughter, her young cousin Emily Smith, 'I get rather tired of people saying "I hope you'll come on the camel" when they ask me out; I feel I've *had* that joke by now.'

Throughout 1957 *The Towers of Trebizond* won success after success, and was awarded a James Tait Black Memorial prize. In America it reached the best-seller lists. Rose seems to have enjoyed the publicity. When she heard that Princess Margaret had been reading bits of *Trebizond* aloud to her friends she wrote to Jean, 'I feel this is real fame, to be read aloud by royalty . . . My head will be quite swollen if this goes on. The Cabinet, the Bench of Bishops, Royalty, half Crockford, a number of the Roman hierarchy – why not the Pope before long? Nasser too, I hope, and possibly Krushchev. It might do these last two good.'

Meanwhile, and during the two years that followed *Trebizond*'s publication – the last two years of Rose's life – her ideas for another novel were taking shape. 'I think I shall write only novels in future', she told Father Johnson. 'It seems less trouble, and if one stays out of novels for some years it is bad for one's sales.' Only a first chapter of the book which she thought of calling *Venice Besieged* was on paper when she died, but she had made quite a few miscellaneous notes. These are of interest as showing how, at this final stage of her career as a writer, she set about bringing together the material for a novel.[1] Evidently much of the action was to take place in Venice – a city Rose loved very dearly – action interspersed with gay dialogue but permeated by a sense of impending doom. Disaster on the grand scale was indeed to occur: a gigantic tidal wave was to sweep in from the Adriatic, engulfing the lagoon islands and swirling over the city, sweeping with it a tide of victims and wreckage. The young heroine however, so Rose confided to one or two of her friends, was to make her escape in fantastic style; when carried by the deluge to its high-water mark, half-way up the façade of Saint Mark's, she was to fulfil a secret ambition by scrambling up on to the back of one of the bronze horses. And thence, from her safe perch, she was to witness the water's gradual ebb.

Superficially the new book would have had no connection with *Trebizond*. Rose had reverted to the third person and there was a fresh set of characters. Yet one may argue that at a less obvious level it might well, in a sense, have been a sequel, since *Venice Besieged* was to begin, as *Trebizond* ended, with a fatal road accident. And the notes show that Rose was still preoccupied with the theme of conscience and guilt, though she was now considering it not only in terms of the individual but in the wider context of mankind encompassed by the powers of spiritual evil. How then might *Venice Besieged* have developed? The following

[1] The first chapter of *Venice Besieged* and also the notes were published as an appendix to a collection of R.M.'s letters to Jean (*Letters to a Sister*, 1964).

lines from Henry Vaughan, transcribed by Rose among her notes, raise a tentative hope that its ending might have been a happy one. Not of course a conventional 'happy ending' but an ending imbued with the joy of Christian reconciliation.

> Taking the curse upon Thy self, so to destroy
> The knots we tyed . . .
> So let Thy grace now make the way
> Even for Thy love . . .

19

DAME ROSE

'A PECULIAR THING is going to occur to me', Rose wrote to a friend[1] a few days before the publication of the 1958 New Year's Honours. 'I am to be made a Dame Commander of the British Empire; for short, a Dame! . . . It seems it was Mr Macmillan's personal idea, as he likes my books . . . I felt very doubtful about accepting it, and consulted Raymond Mortimer, who was so convinced that I ought [to] . . . to encourage them to make more literary Dames . . . that I finally said all right . . . The only other *literary* Dame at present is Edith Sitwell; the others are either actresses or ballet dancers (Margot Fonteyn) or have rendered some service to the State . . . I shall feel and look pretty silly; but I suppose I shall live it down in time. "Dame Rose Macaulay" – dear me!! I shall feel "this is none of I".'

Years earlier, in the 1930s, Rose had looked upon Honours Lists as something to be avoided, and had declined a C.B.E., believing it would bind her to some kind of conformity or at any rate prevent her from feeling free to criticise authority. But since then her attitude had changed and she was thrilled when in 1956 Jean was awarded an M.B.E. for her lifelong work in district nursing. Yet even now she felt diffident about accepting an official honour, and afraid that her friends might think the title 'Dame' ridiculous. 'I fear I have joined "the Establishment",' she told John Hayward when she thanked him for his congratulations. 'I wrote back very cagily at first, asking if I could perhaps commute for some [other] letters referring to the British Empire, but

[1] A young German diplomat named Helmut Rückriegel.

was told no, such quotas being already full. So I settled for the Dame, and here I am, feeling most strange.'

Telegrams and letters poured in, and at the end of the first week in January Rose reported in happy surprise to Jean that she had 'bagged' four bishops, two ambassadors, and most of her 'literary colleagues'. One letter that pleased her especially was from E. M. Forster; he had said frankly but without scorn that 'Dame' was a silly title. 'Yes, indeed, what a silly title', she replied. 'I feel doubtful whether to be a widow Twankey, or an old crone brewing a potion of green herbs on her cottage hob, muttering suitable spells the while – I think I shall opt for the former. Just as, had I been knighted, I should [have] take[n] the role of the White Knight . . . I hope people won't use "Dame" now on my envelopes . . . I prefer "Miss", that has served me all these years, and why should I desert it in my old age?'

Rose was now seventy-six but she did not seem old, for she possessed to a remarkable degree the quality of agelessness. One of her younger Anglican friends, Jacobine Sackville-West, was struck by this when Rose came to tea with her one day in 1958, and spent most of the time on the floor, playing with the three Sackville-West children. 'As I watched her playing with them, I could see that neither she nor they were aware of any difference in age. I think that was one of the wonderful things about her: the way she had of meeting people on their own ground, without ever becoming less than herself.'

Another of the 'wonderful things' about Rose, during this final stage of her life, was the spirit of gaiety which was one of the fruits of her revivified faith. Harold Nicolson made mention of this when after her death he reviewed the first volume of her letters to Father Johnson: 'Her joyous faith halved half her worries and doubled all her joys.' And it was the 'richness and gaiety' of her letters, so he maintained, that left such a deep impression even on 'pagans' such as himself.

By 1958 most of Rose's friends had come to realise, or at least to guess, how much her religion meant to her. But few of them knew that she began each day with Holy Communion at Grosvenor Chapel or St Paul's Knightsbridge, and that she regularly attended retreats, often at Pleshey when the conductor was the Bishop of Tewkesbury (Jock Henderson)[1] who for some years now had been her confessor. Nor were many people aware that she was in much demand for church meetings of various kinds (she spoke, for instance, at a religious Brains Trust at Bognor Regis, and shocked some of the audience by her advocacy of intercommunion, a matter on which she felt strongly). But what all her friends did know, and what they treasured with delight, was that this ageless, amusing, lovable, inexhaustibly kind Rose entered wholeheartedly into their lives and enjoyed their parties. During those last years of her life Rose was very greatly beloved.

Her behaviour as a motorist was perhaps her only habit on which most of her friends had reservations. To quote Harold Nicolson again: 'She would drive in her old battered car through the streets of London, spreading panic right and left, and leaving her passengers with an abiding ache of fear ... Her prowess as a driver was the only one of her gifts in regard to which she was both heartless and conceited.' But this last remark is not quite fair. An interesting passage in one of Rose's letters to Dorothea Conybeare, written in 1956, shows that she was not so insensitive to the dangers of her driving as some supposed: 'How extraordinary life is, isn't it. One slip or stumble, and one is precipitated into months and years of illness; I mean, so much from so little. I feel it when driving my car; one small swerve or miscalculation of space, and the car is smashed and perhaps life lost. I suppose the wonder is that we survive, and our cars, for as long as we do, being so beset with dangers.'

In the spring of 1958 Rose had a fairly serious accident, but not when she was driving. It was in fact caused by a 'slip or stumble',

[1] Now Bishop of Bath and Wells.

and it occurred just after she and Father Denis Marsh, the Anglican Franciscan, had been lunching at St Anne's House in Soho with Patrick McLaughlin. After lunch, as they came out, Rose missed her footing at the top of a steep flight of steps leading down to the street, and crashed to the pavement, fracturing a thigh and a wrist. Father Denis has vivid memories of the incident; he recalls that he made a point of preceding Rose through the door at the top of the steps, because he knew the dangers and wanted to make things easier for her. But she mistook his gesture for rudeness. 'Do friars always push in front of elderly female writers?' she asked. Feeling slightly annoyed he then stood aside, and Rose passed ahead and fell straight down the steps. There was an uproar among the passers-by and Patrick McLaughlin exclaimed 'My God, we've killed her!' 'Don't be ridiculous', came Rose's voice. 'Call an ambulance.' Later, when she and Father Denis were discussing the circumstances of her fall, she was in a mischievous mood. 'Some people', she said, 'say you pushed me down. You didn't, did you?'

After the accident Rose was in hospital for six weeks, but her fractures mended well, and during the summer she was about again, weekending in Dorset, as she often did, with Raymond Mortimer and his friends, taking part in one of the BBC's *Frankly Speaking* programmes, which meant submitting to three interrogators for almost half an hour, and attending a garden party at Lambeth Palace in honour of visiting bishops. Another garden party that summer was an occasion when her new title led to some shamefaced confusion for one of her friends, Laurie Lee. At the end of the afternoon he suddenly realised that he had been introducing her to everyone as 'Dame Edith'. In response to his spluttering apologies Rose was very gracious. 'All Dames are Edith', she observed. 'It's just that some are more Edith than others.'

Then at the end of August she set off on a cruise to the Aegean and the Black Sea. For her it was 'an enchanted voyage', and

Trebizond 'like coming home'. One of the lecturers on the cruise, Dimitri Obolensky, remembers her saying to him 'I would like to die there'.

For quite a time Rose had been aware that she would die in 1958. In 1955 she had written, quite matter-of-factly, to Jean, 'I have an intuition that I shall die in three years, i.e. in 1958, so must bustle about and do a lot of things in the time. When do *you* expect to push off? My own death is very credible to me now, though it usedn't to be. I must go before you, as it will be my turn first; also, I couldn't go on without Saturdays at Romford.' Although Rose had so many devoted friends of all ages, the intimate companionship between herself and Jean held a unique place in her life. 'How very lucky it is that you are so near', she wrote in another letter. 'You might be at the other end of England, or in South Africa or somewhere, and then what *should* I do? As it is, provided you live as long as I do, or even longer, it is all right.'

But Rose did not dwell morbidly on death. She was much more concerned with living the remainder of her life. She hoped to emulate Gilbert Murray who, she felt, had set an inspiring example to the old and ageing by continuing 'in full employment' at ninety, instead of 'laying down pen and typewriter and idling.' She had assured him of this in one of her letters. In that same letter she had spoken of the onset of old age in her own life, which in her mid-seventies she was experiencing as a gradual rallentando: 'Actually I think I still do nearly all I ever did in youth; though the physical things less well and fast. Possibly the mental things too, but I still do them. I find I am hampered by slowness in making an effort to write letters, do accounts, tidy my writing table, change the newspaper linings in my drawers, dust my books, and a lot of other tiresome tasks. In fact I often leave them undone, and then everything becomes what it is now the fashion to call a shambles.'

In Rose's letters at this time there are one or two references to the spiritual aspects of death, all of them interesting as showing the state of her beliefs. The fears of hell fire that had earlier haunted her seem to have dissolved, though the concept of God's judgment was very real to her. Before Christmas 1957, her last Christmas, she told Father Johnson that she found Advent 'a very exciting and rather disturbing season . . . [It] makes one think more than ever of the hourly judgment of God on every thing one thinks, says, or does; I suppose the advent of God in this way becomes closer and more apparent the more one lives, unless one goes on ignoring it . . . This, to me, seems to be the Judgment, not any unspecified and dateless Great Day . . . Judgment; coming each morning at Communion, coming whenever one turns one's mind that way, which one ought to do more often.'

She had clear-cut views as to what she *hoped* the after-life would be like for the redeemed. 'Why *do* we pray that "they [the faithful departed] may have rest"?' she had earlier asked Father Johnson. 'Rest is *not* what we shall want, surely, but more scope for work and new knowledge.' Her final words on the matter, written to Dorothea Conybeare only two days before she died, more or less reiterated this, but there was now a new note of humble readiness to accept whatever might be in store for her. 'As to the future life (if any) I think Jean's idea of annihilation and loss of identity is rather dull. I'd much rather retain personal consciousness, and go on working my way through purgatory (whatever that may be) towards God, than be "lost in universal love" . . . But I don't speculate about it much, as I know I shan't get any clue to it.'

Rose died suddenly on Thursday 30 October 1958, stricken by a heart attack. It was exactly the kind of rapid death she had hoped for: she did not have to suffer any 'last illness'. During the preceding week she had had an attack of bronchitis, but that was nothing unusual, and it did not by any means prostrate her. She wrote letters, made notes for a talk on 'Sacrament and Image' that she had promised to give in Cambridge in November, and also went out several times. Four days before she died, on the Monday, her doctor came about the bronchitis and (so she wrote to Jean) he sounded her chest and gave her something for it. 'So', she concluded emphatically, 'I am really all right again.' Yet there is, in this same letter, a hint that she suspected heart trouble. She admitted to Jean that on the day before the onset of the bronchitis she had felt rather exhausted, and had thought that she might be 'breaking up'. But then, she said, the bronchial trouble explained everything.

On the Tuesday she got up and went with friends to a theatre as well as to a cruise reunion. 'I enjoyed both hugely', she wrote next day to one of her cruise friends, Hanns Ebensten. On Wednesday evening she kept another social engagement. She had promised to join a friend who lived nearby, Robert Cecil, for drinks at his flat, to tell him about the cruise. It was on the following morning that her fatal seizure occurred.

There was a private cremation, conducted by Jock Henderson and Patrick McLaughlin, and a week later a Requiem Mass at Grosvenor Chapel. A memorial service was subsequently held at St Paul's Knightsbridge. At Grosvenor Chapel Gerard Irvine, in his address, put into words the sense of incredulity that Rose's friends felt at her absence:

For so many years that gallant, thin, apparently bloodless and yet so tough, so indomitable, figure has been seen at every party, every private view, protest-meeting, cruise, literary luncheon, or ecclesiastical gathering that it is hard for us to believe she is not to be seen at her own memorial service. Indeed one may be sure no appointment less exigent than Death would have kept her away from the company of so many of her friends in whose doings she was always so interested. She would have liked to have met them here.

Some of the obituaries written by her friends were also obviously from the heart, and a quotation from one of them may serve as an appropriate ending to this book. Its final paragraph included with some lines by Elizabeth Wordsworth which, so the writer said, he often used to remember in Rose's company:

> If all the good people were clever
> And all clever people were good
> The world would be nicer than ever
> We thought that it possibly could.

'If everyone were as good as Rose Macaulay', he concluded, 'and also as clever, the world would be a paradise.'

APPENDICES

THE PLEASURES OF KNOWING ROSE MACAULAY

GENEALOGY OF ROSE MACAULAY

BOOKS BY ROSE MACAULAY

INDEX

The Pleasures of Knowing
Rose Macaulay

The following tributes were published in *Encounter* in March 1959, five months after R.M.'s death.

HAROLD NICOLSON

ONE OF the many things that we shall all remember about Rose Macaulay was her combination of opposites. Her frail appearance was contrasted with a physical energy that would shame a heavyweight; her ridicule of the pretentious was mitigated by her cheerful, even merry, acceptance of all human foibles; her fastidiousness, intellectual and social, did not deter her from suffering fools quite gladly, or deriving pleasure from Levantine guides or Black Sea boatmen. Her gift of derision was unfailing, but she never laughed at things so intimate that her perspicacity might wound. She amused everybody and offended no one. In comparison with her, other witty people appeared conceited, snobbish, or harsh. She possessed a naturally Christian soul.

Her penetrating insight into the affectations or falsities of others was formidable and even disconcerting. The equability of her manner often tempted people to vaunt or give themselves away. Suddenly they would observe a sparkle in her eye and their exuberance would collapse. Rarely did she say anything to reveal her contempt for their egoism; we felt that it had been observed and noted and we were usefully crushed. 'You really mean that?' she would ask occasionally; and we would realise that we hadn't meant it in the least, but were merely indulging in an arresting phrase. She was a champion of sincerity and in her presence all our many forms of falsity withered and died.

I have often seen her displeased but never angry. There was an acid element in her intelligence, but it was citrous merely and never poisoned. I remember on one occasion, when she was overwhelmed by her book on ruins, hearing somebody assure her that there was a castle in Cappadocia that she really must visit. 'My book is growing too big as it is', she murmured coldly. 'But unless you go to Cappadocia', the man insisted, having been there himself, 'you will miss some of the strangest ruins in the world.' 'I shall', she replied firmly, 'make it a point to miss many very strange ruins.' There was always something formidable in her prim snubs.

What fascinated me most about Rose Macaulay, apart from the shining arrows of her mind, was her passion for bathing. I remember that once when she was staying with us in the country during those ice-days that mark an English Easter, she manifested a desire to swim. We told her that, apart from the English Channel which was sixteen miles away and cold in April, all we could offer her was our pond. It was a muddy pond, not very deep, and thick with weeds and water-snakes. We told her of these disadvantages. 'Oh, I never mind things like that', she answered, and within ten minutes there she was swimming happily in the viscous pool. She made us all feel middle-aged.

On one occasion, when I was about to embark upon a foreign lecture tour, she was invited by the British Council to assist them in preparing a leaflet which would inform foreigners of who I was and of what I had written. I was embarrassed on hearing of this commission, partly because I felt it absurd to impose upon a busy woman so trivial a task, and partly because I feared that if Rose Macaulay really read my works, especially my earlier works, she would derive therefrom a lasting scorn of my writing. What alarmed me specially was that she insisted on my lending her a novel that I had once written and of which I was deeply ashamed. Yet when she came to study the subject she assured me that it was that very novel that she had enjoyed the most. I am quite sure that she intended no flattery; she had realised, with her sensitive antennae, that I was ashamed of the book, and in her splendid charity, she was seeking to cheer me up. I had always worshipped her intelligence. From that day onwards I also worshipped her kindness of heart.

How often, in these past months, have I heard my friends murmur, 'Dear Rose, how we miss her.' There will be many men and women who will continue to miss her all their lives.

ROSAMOND LEHMANN

ONE OF the links between Rose and myself was the shared passion for swimming. A few years ago she sponsored my membership of the Lansdowne Club – the idea being that we should meet of an afternoon when its subterranean bath was least likely to be populous, and enjoy many a dip together. Alas! Apart from one memorable occasion, these aquatic projects failed to come about. Rose, not I, was always elsewhere: often in the Serpentine, or the Bosphorus, or the Mediterranean sea. But one chilly, soaking summer day we did contrive a rendezvous. After lunching with our publisher, Mark Bonham Carter, we three descended into the echoing, wanly-electrified, deserted concrete pleasure-vault to take the plunge. Presently Rose emerges from her canvas tentings, voluble, in a one-piece striped exiguous bathing suit, her nose, mouth, chin severe, her brow, her ice-blue eyes obliterated beneath a black diving helmet some sizes too large for her. She carries an inflated rubber mattress, and as we advance towards the brink, casts it upon the waters with business-like despatch. The moment after, I am standing alone; she has vanished. Another moment, and her brisk commentary is rattling down as it were from ceiling-level: she has scampered up, up, out, to the outermost verge of the high-diving board. There I still see her figure indomitably poised: androgynous tall figure, flat as a shape cut out in white paper and blacked in to knees and shoulders; gaunt, comical, adorable – heroically topped with an antique martial casque. She is off, she has jumped feet first, clutching her nose; has cleft the chlorinated blue and sunk sheer as a pair of scissors to the very bottom of the white-tiled basin. She takes a long time to come up; indeed (having by now immersed myself with caution) I become slightly alarmed and haul her upwards by the shoulders. She thanks me cheerfully, and paddles round and round, sketching an old-fashioned side-stroke. Mark swims noiseless, watchful, amused, at a discreet distance. I had assumed Rose to be, like myself, an expert swimmer: it is not so. This fanatical amphibian is not at home in water. She explains this to me as if it had never been a bar to full enjoyment. 'I'm the wrong shape, you see – too long, too thin. I never could remain at the correct angle for self-propulsion. Do swing my legs up.' I do so. Down they fall again. Her laughter is so infectious that I laugh too; but I think: She simply isn't *safe*; surely she could just go down and not surface again. How is it that a creature apparently so ill-suited to this element should sport in it so fearlessly? Also, her lips are blue. She clambers on to the mattress, stretches her peeled-wand limbs full length, and allows me to pull her from end to end of the bath. Almost dreamily – for her prim, somehow practical, academic accents had too much wit and crackle ever to sound dreamy – she ejaculates: 'Oh, Rosamond dear, this is extraordinarily pleasant! I feel like Cleopatra in her barge.'

Once, driving down Duke Street in the rush-hour, I was caught in an unparalleled traffic tangle. Obstruction, impotence, rage, hysteria of horns and human yells exploded within, without, on every side. In front of me, a huge lorry at an angle blocked the road junction. Suddenly, rapidly, from behind its inert and monstrous bulk, an unostentatious saloon model car emerged. Forward it darted headlong into non-space: then, as rapidly, reversed itself, withdrew behind the lorry, once more into non-space. A hush fell. Clearly no one could believe their eyes. When finally, somehow, we disembroiled ourselves and I was able to crawl on, I turned to scrutinise the (doubtless abashed) perpetrator of this outrage. It could only be Rose at the wheel; and Rose it was, in a characteristic hat, passing equably to her destination, superlatively unembarrassed. I called out a mock-sarcastic jibe, to tease her; she did not hear.

She was forever in transit, physically, intellectually, spiritually; energetically not eating, not drinking or sleeping, so it seemed; yet such was her transparency and charity of spirit that she seemed universally available to her friends. She has been called child-like; but to me she suggested youth, a girl, of that pure eccentric English breed which perhaps no longer exists, sexless yet not unfeminine, naive yet shrewd; and although romantic, stripped of all veils of self-interest and self-involvement. I cannot write of her tenderness and under-standing of the grief of others, fruit of deep personal suffering triumphantly surmounted. No one had better cause than I to know and value it. Her last letter arrived the morning before the morning of her death. One of the things it discussed was 'our corrupting profession'. I was meditating on her incor-ruptibility when the news reached me. With the first piercing pang came the thought: 'But we have all just seen her, just been talking to her! How like her to slip off and run lightly, unhampered, without backward glance, straight into her death. Straight through it.'

ALAN PRYCE-JONES

'IT WOULD have to be a High Church ape', says Rose over the telephone, 'because it would like the genuflections so.' She is talking about her plans for *The Towers of Trebizond*, and I am trying in vain to catch her attention enough to ask her to luncheon. 'Then would Tuesday be all right?' I ask, more loudly, but Rose only answers with another question, 'And what other things do apes do? It could play the piano, of course, but not the flute, I suppose. It seems a waste. Everybody plays the piano, generally not so well as an ape.'

She herself played as it were, the telephone, and she did it extremely well so long as time were no object. She cannot have telephoned, like other women, from her bed, for she was an early riser. I imagine her bolt upright, excavating the telephone like an archaeologist from masses of books and paper. Even down the wire one could feel her eyes fixed on one: curious serpent's eyes which never lost their dispassion. Indeed, there was something serpentine about her face altogether, even to the slight hiss in her speech.

Not that she was cold-blooded: far from it. For a year or two I was chairman of a committee upon which she sat, and I can remember the extreme vigour of her interventions. Fortified by tomato juice – for she ate and drank very little – she kept us all up to the mark, and was likely to flash out remarks like 'It is stupid to think that just because I never cared to marry I have no experience of life.' Whenever one looked at her one could almost see the tumult going on behind the delicate bones of her head. Fragments of poetry, scraps of history, the behaviour of apes, the no less surprising behaviour of friends, problems in theology and literary tact: they crowded upon her all at once and all the time. When she swam in chilly seas, or rode a wartime bicycle in the London streets ('I never realised that St James's Street is a kind of alp'), or drove alone down the Spanish coast, it must have been in order to still an unceasing appetite for people and books and the ideas which they expressed. She was as thin and neat as an umbrella, and she never appeared hurried or fussed; but equally she never seemed either bored or inert. Almost the last time I saw her we were both sitting in Ivy Compton-Burnett's dining-room, and she was carrying out a firm inquisition upon her hostess's beliefs. 'I cannot understand you, Ivy, a clever woman like you. You have never got the hang of it. Of course, you may perfectly well be right. There may be nothing to believe *in*. Though I don't lose hope.'

Her secret was that every aspect of this world and the next offered her delightful possibilities of discovery. She disliked things to be finally settled, and so she never came to the end either of a subject or a friendship. This meant that her friends devoured her, for she managed to renew them in their own eyes. I can remember being held, late at night, on a doorstep in a draughty autumn while Rose cross-questioned me about myself. And below the surface of this firm old lady – not that one ever thought of her as old – little by little so much tenderness of feeling, so much comprehension came glimmering up through her words that I felt as if she were the one person who exactly understood my own bewilderments. And then she became practical again. 'You'd better give this wretched car a push. The battery has been very sulky all this week.' One pushed and the car jerked in anger. 'See you at Madge's, see you at Honor's, see you at Joan's, and don't forget my Gargoyle party next week.' Nobody ever zig-zagged more, either driving a car or walking through life; yet the essential part of her was perfectly still. And for those who knew her there will always be something absurd rather than sad in the thought that the telephone will ring, but no voice exclaim, 'This is Rose.'

PATRICK KINROSS

When, a few days before this last Christmas, a card arrived from Rose, it conveyed, somehow, no sense of shock or surprise. How like Rose, one smiled, to send out a last Christmas card after her death! It seemed a natural symbol of continuity, bridging the gap, helping to eliminate the sense of loss, just as her memorial service had done, musical and unmournful like a last party to her friends, as she had planned it to be. Whether or not there is a survival of the soul after death, as she always hoped, the life force in her will survive in the memory, continuing to enhance life in her friends, as her presence did before.

Rose loved parties – not as the young do, restless and seeking, nor as the old do, lonely and bored, but because she loved people, moreover loved them not just with the heart but with the mind. She could never be bored. Whatever the company, there was always something, somebody, some idea to kindle her curiosity and arouse her zest. Whatever was said, she loved to listen, amused at the commonplace, stimulated by the new, diverted by the outrageous. Eagerly inspecting the flat of a new friend, she looked into his wardrobe and exclaimed,

'Oh! So you're one of these young men who like leather jackets. Do put one on for me!'

She hated to forgo a party, with its promise of human experiences. 'I think I'd better not', she would reply to an invitation. 'I've got something else on that evening, and I'm not supposed to be well.' But a few days later she would telephone, 'May I come after all? I seem to be perfectly all right.' She was seldom, in her late seventies, perfectly all right. Sometimes she would go suddenly dizzy and pale, needing but never requesting support. But a sniff of smelling salts, the good old Victorian remedy, would revive her, and she would return to the crowd.

Her misadventures, such was her sense of fun, became adventures. I remember an afternoon of high comedy when she came to Sunday lunch, bubbling over not with annoyance but with amusement at the fact that the water, for some unexplained reason, had failed to flow in her flat, and she could not expect a drop more until Monday. Evelyn Waugh was there, and Henry Green, who had served in the Fire Service during the war and had written of it after, hence should know of these things. So at least challenged Evelyn. Henry, responding, put through a call to the Water Board, and asked knowingly for 'Turn Cock'. He got no satisfaction, so the three of them drove off after lunch, driven by Rose in her car, to her flat. They clambered all over the roof, these three notable authors, over the slippery slates amid the London grime, and located the cistern, which was approached by a steep iron ladder. Rose, as Evelyn recalled, 'shinned up it like a monkey.' The two younger ones followed her, with more circumspection. But nothing, despite Henry's professional experience, could be done. So they went down to the flat – that flat so disorderly in its clutter of pictures and objects and books, but so personal, since she had chosen and loved and lived with each one. Here they found that the water was running again. Turn Cock had turned up after all.

This car of Rose's, usually an obsolete model, became part of her personality, like the things in the flat. She endowed it with anthropomorphic qualities, giving it its head, like a horse, on familiar routes. One night, during a period of petrol rationing, she insisted, despite my protests, on driving me home. Absently she made as if to turn to the right, then pulled the wheel over abruptly like a rein, remarking, 'It must have thought it was going home.' In earlier days she had a similar affection for her bicycle. A friend remembers how, as a young publisher, he came down to the front door of his office to greet Michael Arlen, resplendent in a sleek Rolls-Royce by the kerb. At that moment Rose pedalled up on her ramshackle bicycle, just behind it. The publisher went to her assistance, and together, chuckling at the incongruity, they carried the bicycle into the hall. That started a thirty years' friendship.

Rose was extraordinarily modest. When, on her last cruise to the Black Sea, she was shown to her cabin, she noticed a bouquet of flowers there, wrapped in cellophane, and drew back, saying, 'This must be the wrong cabin. These can't be for me.' Before her first trip to Turkey I gave her an introduction to some friends in Smyrna, who were anxious to meet her and invite her to stay. But modestly, reluctant to bother them with a stranger, she went to a cheap hotel, sending them a message next morning, with a profuse apology for the trouble, asking for the loan of a thermometer, as she did not feel well.

Rose loved to dispute, in a frank and witty and provocative way, about the religious beliefs which one held. Lying in hospital, she broached the topic with an Irish nurse, a Roman Catholic, who declared that at Lourdes she had seen an effigy of the Virgin, shedding living tears – a phenomenon attested, she further declared, by a leading French doctor. 'What things people will believe!' laughed Rose to a visiting friend. I remember a stimulating evening when she expounded her Anglican faith to a sceptical and argumentative Orthodox Jew.

She had about her, perhaps, with her sense of historical continuity, something of the Pantheist – as that last Christmas card, showing the Parthenon successively as the temple of Athena, a Byzantine church, a Turkish mosque, and a sight for tourists, suggested. 'Has it been improved or damaged by all the work done on it down the ages?' she wrote in one of her last articles.[1] 'I myself feel a nostalgia for its mosque and minaret days, but then I have a passion for *mélange* and the fantastically impure ... Apollo into Christ, Artemis into Madonna, rectangle into dome, representational into hieratic, the emergence in golden mosaic of "Almighty God, gloomy, but with an expression of power," and of Our Lady and all the saints.' That card is an appropriate epitaph.

C. V. WEDGWOOD

I FIRST MET Rose in the war, when we both spent much of our leisure reading in the British Museum. 'Come and have a Young Woman's Christian lunch with me', she said one day, over the catalogues, and immensely flattered I queued with her at the neighbouring Y.W.C.A. canteen talking of poetry, bombs, and book reviewing. After that she came often to tea with me at the house I shared with Jacqueline and Philip Hope-Wallace: she always scrupulously and quite unnecessarily brought her own milk-ration. The joint friendship lasted for the rest of her life. No party we gave seemed complete without her, and the upright, uncompromising horse-hair sofa, on which she invariably chose to sit, disregarding all more comfortable chairs, was always the centre of the room.

Rose was one of the few people I have known who could talk, think, and discuss as naturally on the telephone as face to face. Telephone conversations with her play a large part in my memories; the whole of her active, original

[1] 'The New Argonauts' in *The Queen*, 30 September 1958.

mind and the edge of her wit then seemed concentrated in the disembodied voice. We shared a devotion to the 17th century and she would often ring up to settle some minor point. 'Who said Presbyterianism was no religion for a gentleman ?' – not that I could always answer – but speculation and association would carry us by way of the Smectymnuus controversy to the Latin poems of Milton, on through the labyrinth of the Thomason Tracts, with a side glance at an obscure point in the Laudian liturgy and out into the sunlight of Herrick's *Noble Numbers*, with incidental intelligence about mutual friends and the relative state of our work exchanged *en route*: all of this on her part fluent, expert, easy, as though these were the most natural things in the world to discuss over the telephone – as indeed with her they were.

A great place for chance meetings with Rose was the London Library, especially when she was reading for her Portugal book and her *Pleasure of Ruins* – during the work on this book she was at one time in danger of burying herself under the avalanche of her own notes and knowledge from so many different sources. Turning a dark corner among the bookstacks, one would come suddenly upon Rose squatting – an awkward position for one so tall, but squat she certainly did – in a narrow cleft between the shelves with an enormous tome open on her knees. She liked to fetch her own books, however remote or unreachable. In one part of the library precipitous ladders provided a short-cut from one floor to the next. Notices attached to them directed members to the stairs and informed them that they used the ladders at their own risk. Perhaps the idea of risk appealed to that streak of romantic daring in Rose's nature, or perhaps she just wanted to get to the books by the quickest possible route: whatever the reason she was for ever up and down those ladders like a chamois, until the library suppressed them – possibly, as I have always suspected, out of anxiety for the safety of one of their most distinguished members.

MARK BONHAM CARTER

IT WAS AS her publisher that I first met Rose Macaulay. She remains in my memory an unchanging figure, frail and of an almost diaphanous texture, with a look of '*la Vieille Dame*' in the Babar books, of unknown antiquity and unvarying gaiety and zest.

Our communications ran a consistent course whether or not a novel was imminent. Indeed, with Rose, a novel was always imminent, though since the war she only published two, *The World my Wilderness* (1950) and *The Towers of Trebizond* (1956). But she always had a novel in mind even if its progress was interrupted by a book on ruins or an article to finance a voyage or a review for the *Times Literary Supplement* which she could not resist. She told me that her novels started with places – the blitzed ruins of London, Trebizond, or Venice about to be inundated which was the subject she had in mind when she died. The place having been selected, she populated it with appropriate characters. I never saw a novel of hers in manuscript, but she said she wrote them in the back of laundry books on journeys and then typed them out. The first I saw of a novel by Rose was in typescript and with the typescript came an eager demand for criticism and comment.

This request always made me feel somewhat inadequate. For one thing there was very little to be done with Rose's novels. There they stand, one aspect of her personality in print (I have never thought that the novel form was altogether appropriate to her gifts), and by the time they reached her publisher's desk I very much doubt if she could have altered them to any advantage. She wanted to be told that the book was good and she liked to discuss at considerable length on the telephone, on postcards, and over meals various apparently minor problems which arose. In the case of *The Towers of Trebizond* the name of the narrator was the source of much argument. The whole point, she argued, was that no one should know Vere's sex. The name was changed almost weekly from Vicky to Nicky to Evelyn to Vere, and at one time it seemed that in writing the book Rose's main purpose was to confuse the reader on this point. By the reader, she really meant the reviewer. The blurb had to be carefully drafted so that no clue should be given, and when the Book Society made it their monthly choice, I was told to persuade them to preserve a similar discretion in their appreciation. She was always much concerned with what appeared on the dust-jacket. She did not like picture covers though she sometimes produced one of her own rather small and very crowded drawings for this purpose. She detested being described as 'witty' and quotations which employed this adjective were on her Index. With *Trebizond*, there was the problem of the Imprimatur. This read:

> *Nihil Obstat*
> ✠ Raymond Long Crichel
> *Imprimatur*
> Johannes Betjeman, *Decanus*

It was in her view a good joke, and none of her Roman Catholic friends thought it in bad taste. Would we include it? Eventually it was printed in a limited number of copies for distribution to her friends.

As the date of publication approached reviews became an urgent preoccupation. Though she pretended to be indifferent, Rose was deeply concerned about how her books were received and if a critical review appeared she minded very much. Sales did not seem to matter to her, opinions did. In the case of *Trebizond*, she was particularly concerned that one reviewer in particular should not receive the book. He had come to one of her parties unasked and really she did not know him. He had rung her up, she told me, and said: 'Is that Rose?' to which she replied, 'Yes, but who are you?' 'John', he answered. 'Well', said Rose, 'you aren't John Betjeman, and you aren't John Raymond, and you aren't John Metcalf, and you aren't John Lehmann,' and put down the receiver. This was the kind of behaviour that gave her a reputation of being formidable, as indeed she was. Though she enjoyed delivering this crushing blow so unwisely provoked and though she judged it well deserved, she was none the less anxious lest this easy victory produce an unfavourable review. The reviewer in question – such is my ineptitude in these matters – received the book and reviewed it very well. Rose's conscience pricked.

I saw a great deal of her. We lunched regularly, she came to every party we gave at Collins, arriving punctually at six p.m. and staying till the end, and she was at every literary party to which I went. She came to dine with us at Victoria Road and on occasion I had breakfast with her at the Lansdowne Club. When I was married she gave a luncheon there for my wife and me. She asked an enjoyable group of friends, various literary and clerical lights including Rosamond Lehmann. She had instructed everyone to bring a bathing dress. Only Rosamond and I obeyed, and after lunch together with Rose we went down to that subterranean swimming bath where we found one companion who was clearly training to swim the Channel. Rosamond moved about the surface of the water like a stately Spanish galleon or a beautiful water lily transplanted from its natural habitat, while Rose, a two-dimensional figure in a black bathing dress, shot down the chute again and again and urged us to race her across the bath.

Rose compiled an anthology called *Personal Pleasures*. Another anthology could be compiled called *The Pleasures of Knowing Rose Macaulay*. It would be a long anthology and would include sections devoted to her many qualities. Pride of place would go to Integrity. If before she died I had been asked to define integrity to some moral moron, perhaps to one of those who robbed her flat and knocked her down a year or two ago, or to a man from Mars, I would have arranged for him to meet Rose Macaulay.

ANTHONY POWELL

NOT LONG after the war we gave a party and the French husband of our 'daily' came in to help wash the glasses.

'Who was the lady who chained her bicycle to the area railings?' he asked afterwards, rightly suspecting that he was on the track of some new form of English eccentricity.

Rose was known to be addicted to this practice, somehow reminiscent – vicariously through a machine – of the former demonstrations of militant suffragettes. He was told her name.

'Ah', he said, 'if only I had known you were going to invite Miss Macaulay I could have brought *Potterism* with me and she could have signed it.'

After hearing who she was, the fettered bicycle seemed to cause him no further surprise. His familiarity with her novels well suggests the wide range of her literary popularity.

I met Rose first when I was about twenty and found her, at immediate impact, prim, academic, rather alarming. I believe she expressed disapproval of the works of Ronald Firbank. It all seemed very chilly and Cambridge. Nothing could, of course, have been further from a true assessment of her character. So far from being prim, she was prepared to consider all human behaviour with the coolest of judgments. All the same, the suspicion was permissible to those who did not already know her; and she would thoroughly have enjoyed being thought Cambridge.

Much later, referring to some recently published novel – perhaps *A Handful of Dust* – she said to me: 'I have not yet read it. Not a very interesting subject – adultery in Mayfair.'

'Why should you think that uninteresting?'

'You are quite right', she said, 'it was a silly thing to say. Subjects are entirely a matter of how they are treated by the novelist.'

A word should certainly be allowed to her extraordinary Christmas cards, designed by herself, though executed by some hand more proficient in drawing and embellished with Latin verses of her own contrivance. It was at times not at all easy to guess their precise meaning, and perhaps those who traffic in such matters will one day produce a psychological work on them to explain her character and philosophy of life. There was usually about the pictures some suggestion of her own enjoyment in swimming and driving, the last taste, I remember on one occasion, unhindered by a pea-soup London fog. Rather basely, we preferred to leave the car and walk.

You felt with Rose that there was no one on earth she would not stand up to, once she had made up her mind on some subject. She would describe how, arriving in the remote villages of alien countries, she might at times be greeted with a shower of stones by those who took her for a witch. So far as one could gather, such a reception did not daunt her in the least. In fact, she said she liked it, because the same thing had happened to Pliny. Perhaps she was a witch – a White Witch.

Latterly she gave the impression of a being who has cast off already much of material things, one who might suddenly float like gauze away towards the distant horizon. I last saw her in the summer of 1958 at Venice, where a congress of European intellectuals was in progress on the island of San Giorgio.

'What on earth are *you* doing here?'

'I might well ask you the same question.'

'Oh, me?' she said, 'I'm just on my way to the Black Sea.'

WILLIAM PLOMER

ROSE WAS once giving me a spirited ride in her car down the Tottenham Court Road when a full-grown elephant emerged from Torrington Place. An unusual collision seemed imminent. There was no collision: wherever Rose drove she seemed to carry an extra passenger – her guardian angel. But this functionary seemed to be off duty on another day in the vicinity, when we came out of a restaurant after lunch and found three policemen assembled beside her car. Her reasonable but rapid protestations about the harmlessness and even inevitability of her choice of a parking-place were soon overborne, and as we drove away she contemplated a speech in court in her own defence.

I went to court with her, just in case the support of a witness might be helpful. The magistrate, a quiet, fatherly type, looked more willing to try and understand than to condemn, but he seemed a little hard of hearing. Adjusting his spectacles, he contemplated from a distance the frail-looking offender. When asked to plead guilty or not guilty, Rose pleaded guilty with a good many modifications, none of them audible.

'Speak up, Mrs Macaulay!' said the magistrate encouragingly, as he cupped a patient hand over his ear.

Several hundred more words dissolved in the stale and static air.

'Am I to understand, then, that you do in fact plead guilty, Mrs Macaulay? That is what we are trying to arrive at. If you have anything else to say, you will have a chance to speak when we have heard the evidence.'

After we had heard the evidence:

'Well, you have heard what the officer said, Mrs Macaulay. Is there anything else you want to say?'

There was something else. With a strained look of considerate curiosity the magistrate actually bent his ear forward with his hand, like a small shutter on a hinge. I think neither he nor anybody else present caught more than a phrase or two of what seemed to be a voluble but reasoned claim for a degree of civil liberties, particularly for the lack of subversive intention in wishing to park one's car within walking distance of one's eating-place.

'Very well. But you have heard what the officer said.' Then, in a cheerful tone, 'Pay ten shillings, Mrs Macaulay.'

The law-abiding person who would not take the good sense of the law for granted was the same who once expressed, I remember, a strong distaste for the word 'leader,' applied by somebody to the most conspicuous politician of the day.

'Must you call him a *leader*? I don't like that word. Hitler used to be called a leader, if you remember. Don't we all remember? I don't want a leader, do you? Do you feel you need a leader? I don't think I do. I like to think I'm capable of leading myself.'

That capability, so wonderfully mixed with modesty, energy, and a sense of fun, caused her to lead herself to an understanding that membership of the Church of England was compatible with her liberalism, her traditionalism, her questioning mind, and her natural and no doubt inculcated piety. The last time but one that I heard her was in a broadcast interview. After defining her own faith she finely denied that to hold another was to be in outer darkness: all faiths were valuable as different ways of getting at truth.

The last time I saw her was in the house of Canon Collins after Paul Robeson had sung at evensong in St Paul's. I introduced Robeson to her, and the extreme physical contrast between her wan fragility and his great stature was forgotten in the resemblance, the humanity, of their respective ways of looking at life.

DIANA COOPER

'ROSE, ROSE, ROSE, ROSE, shall I never see thee more?' So went the glee we sang in childhood, and this catch caught at my heart when I heard of the death of one whom I had only known a few weeks, yet whom I loved with an enthusiasm that quite possessed me.

I knew, when I first met Rose Macaulay at some gathering of friends, that I wanted to please her and shine for her, and that she would sharpen my bluntness. Because of this fervent admiration I leapt at the suggestion of joining a ship on which she was sailing, bound for Greece and a tour of the Crimean and Turkish coasts. Rose, the keenest of the passengers, was looking forward to this cruise and was to love and live it more than any. A few weeks before we embarked she had broken her hip and her hand, but as her bones like her spirit had lost no sap or spring of youth, and as her weight was negligible, she seemed not to remember the accident. The arenas and eminences of Delphi, our first stop, she scaled with no totter. 'Don't photograph me in ruins', she said, and we obeyed. In the temple of Aegina – reached on a donkey she chose from a herd as being the likeliest – she bestrode the highest points of pediments. Neither amused nor impressed by her own unusualness she swam our many Hellesponts, not as an ageing woman managing splendidly but as part of the beauty and the tide.

I remember the acuteness of her disappointment when she did not draw a place for a desperate expedition to Baskiserail: it entailed six hours of precipice-driving in a bus after dark, a brief visit at dawn to the crumbles of a Tartar city, a night in what the guide-book called 'a wretched kahn', and an admission by the Russians of its being 'extremely primitive' – six in a bed. 'I shall take a droshky', said Rose. Did she visualise a taxi, or a troika? She couldn't say, but her faith she pinned to a droshky. Dressed in her colourless-sparrow's garb, a well-secured toque, a basket, and a crook, I saw her stump off indomitably to a bus-seat gladly resigned by a less intrepid traveller. I was limping behind with an extra jersey and a deck-chair mattress to make her independent of beds of Ware; but she would have none of them – 'This is very warm', she said, finger-ing her brindle-cotton jacket, 'I'll be like the others.'

The tedium of a day at sea was relieved by a Brains Trust. Rose, the Padre, and two others presided over by a Q.C. question-master, were asked if they considered Death preferable to Dishonour. The Padre led off, his cloth harnessing him to the classic reply that Belief making Death so happy what hesitation could there be? This was not in the mood of the listeners, who felt uneasy. But Rose, the last questioned, knew games and how to play them. 'Dishonour every time', she said; 'no question at all – Dishonour.' The team was next asked what other kind of life they could have wished for. 'One with absolute power', said Rose. 'Perhaps an emperor of Trebizond's. Anyway, Absolute Power.'

She had our ship in thrall; we gave her our hearts and peals of laughter. Her manner was not gay – she threw no confetti – but her caustic flares could make us hilarious.

The night before leaving I gave her a close little hat filmy with ashen veil; though sober enough, I felt it to be too girlish for me. She seemed pleased out of all proportion. Did she wear it, I wonder, and remember her ardently admiring friend who now feels unkindly robbed of new-found and still uncounted treasure?

Genealogy of Rose Macaulay

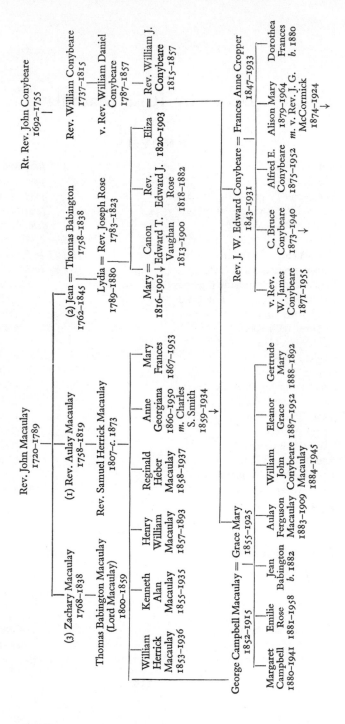

Books by Rose Macaulay

NOVELS

Abbots Verney	*John Murray*	1906
The Furnace	*John Murray*	1907
The Secret River	*John Murray*	1909
The Valley Captives	*John Murray*	1911
Views and Vagabonds	*John Murray*	1912
The Lee Shore	*Hodder & Stoughton*	1912
The Making of a Bigot	*Hodder & Stoughton*	1914
Non-Combatants and Others	*Hodder & Stoughton*	1916
What Not: A Prophetic Comedy	*Constable*	1918
Potterism: a Tragi-farcical Tract	*Collins*	1920
Dangerous Ages	*Collins*	1921
Mystery at Geneva	*Collins*	1922
Told by an Idiot	*Collins*	1923
Orphan Island	*Collins*	1924
Crewe Train	*Collins*	1926
Keeping up Appearances	*Collins*	1928
Staying with Relations	*Collins*	1930
They Were Defeated	*Collins*	1932
Going Abroad	*Collins*	1934
I Would be Private	*Collins*	1937
And No Man's Wit	*Collins*	1940
The World my Wilderness	*Collins*	1950
The Towers of Trebizond	*Collins*	1956

POETRY

The Two Blind Countries	*Sidgwick & Jackson*	1914
Three Days	*Constable*	1919

ESSAYS, CRITICISM, ETC.

A Casual Commentary	*Methuen*	1925
Catchwords and Claptrap	*Hogarth Press*	1926
Some Religious Elements in English Literature	*Hogarth Press*	1931

Milton	*Duckworth*	1934
Personal Pleasures	*Gollancz*	1935
The Writings of E. M. Forster	*Hogarth Press*	1938

ANTHOLOGY

The Minor Pleasures of Life	*Gollancz*	1934

HISTORY AND TRAVEL

Life Among the English	*Collins*	1942
They Went to Portugal	*Jonathan Cape*	1946
Fabled Shore: from the Pyrenees to Portugal	*Hamish Hamilton*	1949
Pleasure of Ruins	*Weidenfeld & Nicolson*	1953

LETTERS

Letters to a Friend: 1950–1952	*Collins*	1961
Last Letters to a Friend: 1952–1958	*Collins*	1962
Letters to a Sister	*Collins*	1964

INDEX